# AMORITES AND
# CANAANITES

# AMORITES AND CANAANITES

BY

## KATHLEEN M. KENYON

C.B.E., D.Litt.

FELLOW OF THE ACADEMY

THE SCHWEICH LECTURES
OF THE BRITISH ACADEMY
1963

LONDON
PUBLISHED FOR THE BRITISH ACADEMY
THE OXFORD UNIVERSITY PRESS
1966

*Oxford University Press, Ely House, London W. 1*

GLASGOW NEW YORK TORONTO MELBOURNE WELLINGTON
CAPE TOWN SALISBURY IBADAN NAIROBI LUSAKA ADDIS ABABA
BOMBAY CALCUTTA MADRAS KARACHI LAHORE DACCA
KUALA LUMPUR HONG KONG

PRINTED IN GREAT BRITAIN
AT THE UNIVERSITY PRESS, OXFORD
BY VIVIAN RIDLER
PRINTER TO THE UNIVERSITY

# PREFACE

THIS volume is the text upon which the Schweich Lectures given in November 1963 were based. It is an attempt to assemble the archaeological evidence concerning the inhabitants of Palestine up to the period of the entry of the Israelites. The material used is almost entirely archaeological. It is not intended to suggest that this is the only material that bears on the problem. But the archaeological material has been far less studied than the textual. Much of it has only accumulated in recent years, and no previous attempt has been made to produce a coherent picture of the material evidence of the culture of the Syro-Palestine coastal area for the thousand years or so preceding the entry of the Israelites into Palestine. For Palestine itself, the evidence is abundant. But this evidence makes it clear that the origins of the culture must be sought to the north and east. Here the evidence is much less abundant and much less coherent. The present volume seeks to draw it together and to relate it to the Palestine evidence.

It is, moreover, in Syria that written history touches the peoples of whom the material culture is the evidence. The deductions to be drawn from the written history as at present known are set out in Chapter XXI of the revised edition of the *Cambridge Ancient History*, and are not dealt with here. The broad conclusion is accepted that the disruption of orderly government and town life in the last centuries of the third millennium was the work of the Amorites. Attention has been concentrated on what is the material evidence of the appearance of these groups first in Syria and then in Palestine.

The second part of the study is concerned with the material evidence relating to the Canaanite culture of the coast of Syria and Palestine, and an attempt has been made to show where and when this emerged from the Amorite background. Again the evidence used is archaeological, for this is the evidence common to the whole littoral. The dawn of literature in the Canaanite area is a different and wider study, but it must be emphasized that it is not complete in itself. The evidence provided by archaeology from the material remains is also necessary.

KATHLEEN M. KENYON

*1965*

# CONTENTS

# LIST OF FIGURES IN THE TEXT

# LIST OF PLATES

# ACKNOWLEDGEMENTS

ACKNOWLEDGEMENT for kind permission to reproduce illustrations is made to the following, to whom the copyright of the illustrations belongs:

British School of Archaeology in Jerusalem, Jericho Excavation Fund: Pls. I. 1, 2, II. 2, III. 1, 2, IV. 1, 2, XXII. 1, 2, XXIII. 1, XXVIII. 1, 2, XXIX. 1, 2, XXX. 1, 2; figs. 2, 4, 6, 7, 9, 11, 26, 35, 40.

Oriental Institute of the University of Chicago: Pls. II. 1, V. 1, 2; fig. 17.

Monsieur C. F. A. Schaeffer and the *Mission de Ras Shamra*: Pls. V. 3, VI. 1, 2; figs. 20, 21, 22, 29, 33.

Monsieur M. Dunand: Pls. IX, X, XI. 1, XV, XVI. 1, 2, XVII, XVIII. 1, 2, XIX. 1, 2, XX. 1, 2.

Monsieur P. Montet: Pls. XI. 2, XII, XIII, XIV, XXI. 1, 2.

The Trustees of Sir Henry Wellcome: Pl. XXIII. 2.

British School of Archaeology in Egypt: Pl. XXIV. 1, 2; fig. 37.

Professor Y. Yadin and the James A. de Rothschild Expedition at Hazor: Pl. XXV.

The Editors of *Syria*: Pl. XXVI. 1; figs. 23, 24, 28.

University College, London, Department of Egyptology: Pl. XXVI. 2.

The Trustees of the British Museum: Pl. XXVI. 3; fig. 38.

British School of Archaeology in Jerusalem, Jericho Excavation Fund, and Ernest Benn, Ltd.: Figs. 8, 10, 12, 13, 30, 31, 32, 34, 39.

Ernest Benn, Ltd.: Figs. 5, 14, 15, 16, 18, 19, 25, 27.

# REFERENCES AND ABBREVIATIONS

| | |
|---|---|
| *AASOR* | *Annual of the American Schools of Oriental Research.* New Haven, Conn. |
| *ADAJ* | *Annual of the Department of Antiquities of Jordan.* Amman. |
| *A.G.I,II* | *Ancient Gaza I and II. Tell el Ajjul.* W. M. Flinders Petrie. London, British School of Archaeology in Egypt. 1931, 1932. |
| *APEF* | *Annual of the Palestine Exploration Fund.* London. |
| *A. in H.L.* | *Archaeology in the Holy Land.* Kathleen Kenyon. London, Ernest Benn, Ltd. 1960. |
| *Beit Mirsim, Tell* | *Tell Beit Mirsim I, IA, II. AASOR XII, XIII, XVII.* W. F. Albright. |
| *Beth-pelet* | See *Fara, Tell.* |
| *Beth-shan* | 'Beth-Shan: Earliest Pottery.' G. M. Fitzgerald. *The Museum Journal, Philadelphia,* xxiv. |
| *Byblos I, II* | *Fouilles de Byblos I, II.* M. Dunand. Paris. 1939, 1954. |
| *Byblos et l'Égypte* | *Quatre campagnes de Fouilles à Gebeil. 1921–1922–1923–1924.* P. Montet. Paris, 1928 and 1929. |
| *CAH* | *Cambridge Ancient History.* Revised edition (in progress). |
| *Carchemish II* | *Report on the excavations at Jerablus on behalf of the British Museum. Part II. The Town Defences.* C. L. Woolley. London, British Museum. 1921. |
| *Duweir, Tell* | See *L. IV.* |
| *Eretz Israel* | *Annual of the Israel Exploration Society.* Jerusalem, Israel. |
| *Fara, Tell* | *Beth-pelet I.* W. M. Flinders Petrie. London, British School of Archaeology in Egypt. 1930. *Beth-pelet II.* E. Macdonald, J. L. Starkey, and Lankester Harding. London, British School of Archaeology in Egypt. 1932. |
| *Iraq* | London, British School of Archaeology in Iraq. |
| *Hazor I, II* | *Hazor I. An account of the First Season of Excavations, 1955. Hazor II. An account of the Second Season of Excavations, 1956.* Yigael Yadin *et al.* Jerusalem, Israel, The Hebrew University. 1958 and 1960. |
| *J. I, II* | *Excavations at Jericho. I. The Tombs excavated in 1952–4. II. The Tombs excavated in 1955–8.* Kathleen M. Kenyon. London, British School of Archaeology in Jerusalem. 1960, 1965. |
| *Jericho 1907–1909* | *Jericho. Die Ergebnisse der Ausgrabungen.* E. Sellin and C. Watzinger. Leipzig. 1913. |
| *Joseph to Joshua* | H. H. Rowley. Schweich Lectures for 1948, British Academy. London, Oxford University Press. 1950. |

| | |
|---|---|
| *Khan Sheikhoun* | 'Une Campagne de Fouilles à Khan Sheikhoun.' Le Comte du Mesnil du Buisson. *Syria*, xiii. |
| *LAAA* | *Liverpool Annals of Art and Archaeology*. University of Liverpool. |
| *L. IV* | *Lachish IV (Tell ed-Duweir). The Bronze Age*. Olga Tufnell. London, Oxford University Press. 1958. |
| *M. II* | *Megiddo II: Seasons 1935–39*. G. Loud. Chicago. 1948. |
| *M. Stages* | *Notes on the Chalcolithic and Early Bronze Age Pottery of Megiddo*. R. M. Engberg and G. M. Shipton. *Studies in Ancient Oriental Civilization* 10. Chicago. 1934. |
| *M. Tombs* | *Megiddo Tombs*. P. L. O. Guy and R. M. Engberg. Chicago. 1938. |
| *Oxford Bible Atlas* | Ed. Herbert G. May. Oxford University Press. 1962. |
| *PEQ* | *Palestine Exploration Quarterly*. London, Palestine Exploration Fund. |
| *Qatna* | 'Les Ruines d' el-Mishrifé au Nord-Est de Homs (Émèse).' Le Comte du Mesnil du Buisson. Preliminary reports. *Syria*, vii–ix. |
| *QDAP* | *Quarterly of the Department of Antiquities of Palestine*. Oxford. |
| *Ras Shamra* | Preliminary reports of 1st to 10th seasons. Claude F. A. Schaeffer. *Syria*, x, xii–xx.<br>*Ugaritica II. Mission de Ras Shamra*. Tome V. Claude F. A. Schaeffer. Paris. 1949. |
| *RB* | *Revue Biblique*. École Biblique et Archéologique de St. Étienne, Jerusalem, Jordan. |
| *Stratigraphie comparée* | *Stratigraphie comparée et chronologie de l'Asie occidentale (IIIᵉ et IIᵉ millénaires)*. Claude F. A. Schaeffer. London, Oxford University Press. 1948. |
| *Syria* | Paris, Librairie Orientaliste Paul Geuthner. |
| *Ugaritica* | See *Ras Shamra*. |
| *Yahudiyeh, Tell el* | *Hyksos and Israelite Cities*. W. M. Flinders Petrie. London, British School of Archaeology in Egypt. 1906. |

# INTRODUCTION

## AMORITES AND CANAANITES

'THE Amalekites dwell in the land of Negeb; the Hittites, the Jebusites and the Amorites dwell in the hill country; and the Canaanites dwell by the sea, and along the Jordan.'[1]

Both the Biblical account and the archaeological evidence make it clear that when the Israelites entered into the Promised Land, they took possession of a land already fully occupied. It is not the intention of the present study to consider the stages or chronology of the Israelite infiltration. The evidence for this was fully considered by Professor Rowley in the Schweich Lectures of 1948; recent archaeological work, particularly at Jericho, requires the modification of some of his conclusions, but before it can be superseded as an admirable summary of the available evidence, much more archaeological investigation is required. The object of the present study is to assemble the evidence, primarily archaeological, concerning the history and culture of the peoples that the Israelites found in occupation of the Promised Land, and to assess the effect of this culture upon the infiltrating Israelites.

From the archaeological evidence one can draw a reasonably clear picture as to the peoples of the land. But the archaeological record is always anonymous until a much later period. The archaeologist can, on the evidence assembled over the last forty years, say with complete confidence that a site was occupied in the Middle and Late Bronze Age, covering a period from about 1900 B.C. to 1200 B.C., within which must fall the events covered by the early books of the Old Testament, from the wanderings of the Patriarchs to the entry of the Israelites into the Promised Land. But, in the absence of any inscriptional material, the archaeologist can only establish subdivisions within any one chronological period on the basis of differences in material equipment. For the period in question, the archaeological evidence is clear. The whole of Cisjordan was one cultural province. From Hazor in the north to Lachish in the south, of the sites identifiable in the early Biblical record for which there is archaeological evidence, the uniformity in the material

[1] Numbers xiii. 29.

B

is remarkable. East of the Jordan, the position is different, a subject to which it will be necessary to return.

Yet the books of the Bible dealing with the early stages of the establishment of the Israelites in Palestine continually refer to a number of peoples. Though these books are a later recension of what must be orally transmitted tribal records, details such as these, inapplicable to the later history of Israel, must be accepted as of early origin.[1] In Transjordan, the principal enemy was the Amorites, with a main kingdom between the Arnon and the Jabbok (Numbers xxi. 13) and a northern group in Gilead (Numbers xxxii. 39). In many places the whole of the country west of the Jordan is referred to as the land of Canaan. But the opponents of Israel in this area are listed in the familiar rubric as the Amorites, the Perizzites, the Canaanites, the Hittites, the Girgashites, the Hivites, and the Jebusites (Joshua xxiv. 11).

The importance of these groups is clearly unequal. Some, for instance the Perizzites and the Girgashites, float in a vacuum, unattached to any locality; the Hittites are similarly unattached, and the question whether they are related to the mighty Hittites of the north or whether the name is corrupted, is a subject of debate. The Jebusites would seem in other references to be comprised within the Amorites, for the king of Jerusalem, a town specifically Jebusite in Joshua xv. 63, is one of the kings of the Amorites who banded against the appeasing Gibeonites as described in Joshua x. 5, while the only town ascribed to the Hivites is Gibeon (Joshua xi. 19).

If the overall emphasis of the ascriptions is to be trusted, the major groups are certainly the Amorites and the Canaanites. The solid opposition to the Israelites in Transjordan was Amorite (Numbers xxi. 21–23). The coalition that Joshua is described as defeating at Gibeon, of the kings of Jerusalem, Hebron, Jarmuth, Lachish, and Eglon, was Amorite (Joshua x. 5). It can be inferred that 'Ai was also Amorite on the evidence of Joshua vii. 7. The Canaanites were in the south at Arad in the Negeb (Numbers xxii. 1–3), in the south-east (Joshua xiii. 3), and at Gezer (Joshua xvi. 10); like Gezer, the Canaanite towns of the plain of Esdraelon—Beth-shan, Ibleam, Dor, En-dor, Taanach,

---

[1] Unless it is to be accepted that entry of the Israelites took place after c. 1200 B.C., the references to the Philistines must be insertions reflecting conditions at the time of the recension, and it should be noted that though they are mentioned, for instance in Joshua xiii. 3, there is never any reference to warfare with them at this stage or to driving them out.

and Megiddo, are recorded in Joshua xvii. 11–12 as withstanding the Israelite infiltration, while Hazor 'the head of all those Kingdoms' (Joshua xi. 10) is referred to as Canaanite in Judges iv. 2. Strangely enough, Jericho, though it plays such a prominent part in the account in the Book of Joshua, is not ascribed to any group, though it might be inferred from the general description in Numbers xiii. 29 that 'the Canaanites dwell by the sea and along the Jordan' that it was considered to be Canaanite.

When the towns specifically designated as Amorite and Canaanite are plotted on a map (Fig. 1),[1] the overall pattern, though it has gaps, accords well with the general location of the peoples of the land given in Numbers xiii. 29 which is quoted at the beginning of this section. The inhabitants of the hill-country both to the east and the west of the Jordan were regarded by the Israelites as Amorites, and the inhabitants of the coastal plain, the valley of Esdraelon, and the valley of the Jordan as Canaanites, and so presumably they regarded themselves. The Amorites were hill-dwellers, the Canaanites plain-dwellers.

This would, however, not appear to be the whole picture even from the literary evidence. Though, as has been seen, there is frequent reference to tribal groupings with, west of the Jordan, a geographical core of Amorites surrounded by a bordering area of Canaanites, the country as a whole is unambiguously referred to as Canaan,[2] of which the River Jordan formed the frontier. No all-embracing name is given to Transjordan, but it was clearly considered to be Amorite at least as far north as the Yarmuk. The picture of two cultural provinces divided by the Jordan is that which in fact is given by the archaeological evidence.

The purpose of this study is to discuss the archaeological evidence for the build-up of groups and cultures in Palestine that had produced this composite picture by the time of the entry of the Israelites, which it is almost universally accepted must fall within the archaeological period of the Late Bronze Age, though many scholars would agree that it was a much more complex and prolonged movement than the Biblical account would

---

[1] In the identification of sites, the *Oxford Bible Atlas* has been followed.

[2] e.g. Numbers xxxiii. 51, 'When you pass over the Jordan into the land of Canaan'; Joshua xiv. 1, 'And these are the inheritances which the people of Israel received in the land of Canaan', with the list following covering the whole country.

suggest.[1] The demarcation of the Late Bronze Age from the
Middle Bronze Age is political rather than cultural. The

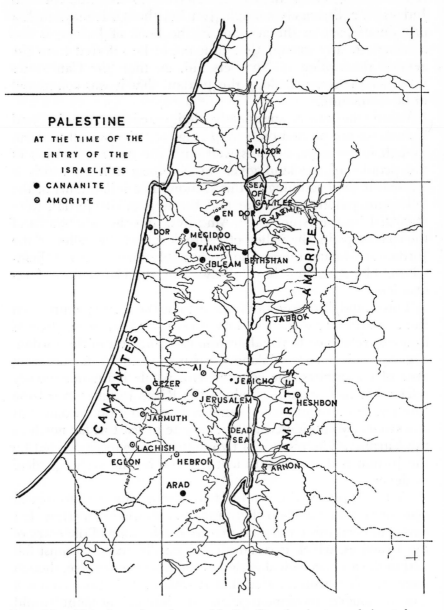

FIG. I. Map of Palestine at time of entry of the Israelites, showing towns designated
Amorite and Canaanite in Biblical sources.

material equipment of the earlier period develops without
break into that of the later. Politically, however, the situation is

[1] e.g. Rowley, *From Joseph to Joshua.*

different, for with the advent of the Egyptian XVIIIth Dynasty, Egypt once more begins to exert influence on the Syrian coast. The expulsion of the Hyksos from Egypt, *c.* 1580–1560 B.C., must have had direct repercussions upon Palestine, for it was in that direction that the Asiatics were thrown out from Egypt, thus adding a further admixture to the population, while the restoration of stable rule in Egypt gave a great stimulus to trade in the Eastern Mediterranean. It is the material evidence of this trade that chiefly differentiates the archaeological finds of the Late Bronze Age from those of the preceding period. In the basic culture there is no break. Again, though *c.* 1200 B.C. can be taken as a convenient point for the beginning of the Iron Age, with the arrival of the Philistines, there is, except on those sites that became Philistine cities, still cultural continuity.

This continuity, from the Middle to the Late Bronze Age and into the Iron Age, is of particular importance, for this is the material culture that the Israelites found in the land. It is, moreover, the culture that they to a large degree adopted. One of the major difficulties in establishing the chronology of the entry of the Israelites is that at no point in a single site can one say that the material evidence shows that a new people had arrived. The ascription of a particular destruction to the Israelites is just a matter of guess-work. Only *c.* 1100 B.C. are there marked innovations in pottery and other objects, and it would be a revolutionary proposition to suggest that this represents the first arrival of the Israelites. Failing this, it must be accepted that all the Israelite groups arrived as essentially nomadic people with very little indeed in the way of material possessions, and that when they settled down they took over the equipment of their predecessors in the land.

It will be shown that the Middle Bronze Age culture of Palestine was essentially Canaanite. In order to establish what this culture was, and its relationship with what went before, it will be necessary to trace the course of events in Palestine in the third and second millennia B.C., and to relate them to what was happening in the rest of the Semitic area of western Asia. As far as Palestine is concerned, this evidence is entirely archaeological, with particular emphasis on pottery, and thus the links with the wider area are also archaeological, though fortunately the picture is here illuminated by documentary evidence.

# I

## THE INTERMEDIATE EARLY BRONZE—
## MIDDLE BRONZE PERIOD IN PALESTINE

### INTRODUCTORY

THE greater part of the fifth and fourth millennia in Palestine is a Dark Age. After the successive Pre-Pottery Neolithic stages with, at least at Jericho, their urban developments, and at that site extending down to a date as yet undefined in the sixth millennium, the succeeding Neolithic and Chalcolithic cultures are retrogressive. Village settlements of no great size are all that are found, and there is no evidence of developed communities, the growth of trade, or even of general cultural progress. The most widespread culture, the Ghassulian of the Jordan Valley and the allied groups, is certainly intrusive, and does not seem to have made any appreciable contribution towards what followed.

The last centuries of the fourth millennium constitute a period in which a number of groups were entering Palestine, presumably from the east and north-east, though little is known of their origins. Their culture was simple, and they settled in groups or combinations of groups, for which most of the evidence is from tombs rather than structures. Their importance is that the sites at which they settled, unlike those occupied by the Ghassulians, became towns in the succeeding phase. It may be that the final impulse towards urbanism came from a final wave of newcomers, but the result was an amalgamation of groups of varying origins out of which the comparatively uniform Early Bronze Age culture of Palestine emerged; the use of the term Proto-Urban for this stage is therefore suggested.[1]

The Early Bronze Age culture of Palestine, lasting from the late fourth millennium to the twenty-third century B.C.,[2] was

---

[1] *Jericho I*, pp. 5 ff; *Jericho II*, pp. 3 ff.

[2] The dating depends on evidence of contacts with Egypt ranging from E.B. II contacts with the Ist Dynasty to E.B. III contacts with the IVth Dynasty. The beginning of the following period must be related to that of the First Intermediate in Egypt, for both tell the same tale of civilizations destroyed by nomads. To these nomadic incursions, from, as will be seen, north-east Syria, the city states of Palestine, comparatively weak and geographically nearer, would have succumbed before Egypt. Therefore, on the chronology accepted in the new edition of the *Cambridge Ancient History*, there is a range of an initial date for E.B. I from before 3100 B.C., to some time before 2181 B.C. for the end of E.B. III. From the point of view of Palestinian archaeology a shorter chronology would be much more acceptable.

essentially one of city states. For the first time, a number of walled towns are found scattered over the country. Each would presumably be the centre of a group of smaller units, very probably with an organization similar to that reflected in the Book of Joshua by the list (Joshua xvii. 11) of the area allocated to Manasseh, 'Beth-shean and its villages, and Ibleam and its villages, and the inhabitants of Dor and its villages . . .'. There is no evidence, literary or archaeological, that any of the towns achieved hegemony, and here Palestine (and the Syrian coast as a whole) lagged behind the great river valleys of Egypt and Mesopotamia, where a unitary control created, out of the similar city states, empires to lead the next step in the progress of civilization.

There is evidence concerning the defences of these towns[1] and of elaborate town planning at least by Early Bronze III.[2] The pottery of the stage and the associated objects are well known. It is presumed that the people were Semites, though direct linguistic evidence is lacking, but the existence of a sanctuary at 'Ai with the triple elements of the later Semitic sanctuaries[3] may be adduced as evidence to support the supposition. The pottery evidence is clear that there are close connexions with the people of the Syrian coastal area; for instance pottery from Byblos[4] is close to that of, for instance, Megiddo and Jericho of E.B. II–III,[5] and pottery from Ras Shamra[6] can be compared with that of T. Beit Mirsim[7] and Jericho[8] of E.B. III. The inhabitants of the Syrian coast in the second millennium were known as Canaanites. But even in Syria it is doubtful whether there is literary evidence to identify the inhabitants at this stage as Canaanites, or, as will be seen, archaeological evidence of continuity that would enable one to carry back the name from the second to the third millennium.

The archaeological evidence would in fact suggest that it was movements of people taking place in the last centuries of the third millennium and the beginning of the second millennium

[1] e.g. T. el Far'ah, *RB* lv, lxix; Jericho, *PEQ* 1953, 1955.

[2] Kenyon, 'Some Notes on the Early and Middle Bronze Strata of Megiddo', *Eretz Israel*, v.

[3] J. Marquet, *Les Fouilles de 'Ay (et-Tell)*, 1933–5.

[4] Dunand, *RB* lix, pls. III–V.

[5] *Jericho I*, figs. 34, 38, 43, 45 &c.; R. M. Engberg and G. M. Shipton, *Notes on the Chalcolithic and Early Bronze Age Pottery of Megiddo*, charts.

[6] *Ugaritica II*, fig. 99. 7–14 = *Stratigraphie comparée*, pl. XIII, 46–50.

[7] Albright, *AASOR* xiii, pl. I, 1–2.

[8] *Jericho I*, figs. 38, 44.

that produced the groupings and cultures found in Syria and Palestine in the second half of the second millennium B.C.

The initial period is that of the great movements that resulted in the break-up of Sumerian rule in Mesopotamia and, at the other end of the Fertile Crescent, the collapse of Old Kingdom Egypt. At least by the time of Sargon of Akkad (2371–2316 B.C.), groups of Amurru were penetrating into Mesopotamia, and by the time of the IIIrd Dynasty of Ur (2113–2004 B.C.) these penetrations were becoming increasingly warlike, culminating in the massive immigrations that preceded the establishment of the Ist Dynasty of Babylon. The Egyptian picture is similar. By the time of the end of the VIth Dynasty (c. 2181 B.C.), the Egyptians were ceasing to go to Byblos to obtain wood and the pine-essence necessary for embalming. In the First Intermediate period, Asiatics and their flocks, clearly nomadic pastoralists, were penetrating into the Delta, and down to the time of the XIIth Dynasty (1991–1786 B.C.) the enemies on the eastern borders of Egypt were Beduin and dwellers in the desert.

The literate peoples of the great river valleys therefore record the growing pressure of nomadic bands, called Amurru by the Sumerians, that were on the move at this period. It is now necessary to see how the archaeological record reflects these events and provides evidence of the material culture. Since the archaeological record for Palestine is relatively much more full, this will be dealt with first.

\*    \*    \*    \*    \*

The use of the term Intermediate Early Bronze—Middle Bronze period in Palestine was first introduced by J. H. Iliffe in his arrangement of objects in the Palestine Archaeological Museum. It covered a period called by Sir Flinders Petrie the Copper Age[1] and by Professor Albright Middle Bronze I.[2] As an objection to the former term, the technological inconsistency that the period certainly follows that called Early Bronze Age can be raised; to the latter term, there is an even more cogent objection in the view, on the Jericho evidence incontrovertible, that the period has even less to do with the rest of the Middle Bronze Age than with the Early Bronze Age. The Jericho evidence is, on the one hand, quite clear that the way of life, the burial customs, the pottery, the tools and weapons are all equally distinct in the Early

[1] *Ancient Gaza II.*                    [2] *AASOR* xii.

Bronze Age, the Intermediate Early Bronze–Middle Bronze period, and the Middle Bronze Age, and on the other that there were sharp stratigraphic breaks between the periods.

The evidence of a stratigraphic break at Jericho at the end of the Early Bronze Age is dramatic. The defences of the Early Bronze Age town had had a chequered life. In one area where a complete cut was made through the defences, seventeen successive stages could be identified. Some of these, but not all (for some of the evidence came from the other side of the trench), are shown on Fig. 2. The final wall was erected hurriedly, with poor foundations and with the use of broken bricks. It was possibly not even completed when it was destroyed by fire. Into its ruins was cut a house quite different in plan from those hitherto found, and built of distinctive greenish bricks. These houses could be traced down the slope of the mound outside the earlier town wall (Pl. I. 1), and it here became clear that they did not immediately succeed the destruction of the wall, for in the ditch belonging to that wall there was a fill containing pottery, here called Intermediate Early Bronze–Middle Bronze, or E.B.–M.B. for short, which had accumulated to a height of about 9 ft. before the first houses were built.

The Early Bronze Age town was thus destroyed and succeeded by something quite different. No trace of a town wall of this period has been found. An early stage of occupation that left no trace of structural remains and was therefore presumably of a camping nature, was succeeded by one in which houses straggled down the slopes of the mound. This latter stage, of which the houses were flimsy and ill planned, is also found on the surrounding hill slopes.

On other sites there is a similar lack of town walls and solid structures, with the single exception of Megiddo. For example, of sites that have produced clear evidence of E.B.–M.B. occupation (Fig. 3), at T. Ajjul only tombs have been found, at T. Beit Mirsim there was no trace of a wall or houses, and some of the population certainly lived in a cave, for only here were intact vessels found, and at T. Duweir again the evidence was mainly from tombs, on a hill-spur some 700 metres north of the tell, and one group lived in a cave situated at a distance of *c.* 600 metres from the tell. This is a remarkable contrast to the compact, closely built-up, walled towns of the Early Bronze, of which T. el Far'ah may be taken as an example.

The burial customs show the same sharp distinction. The typical tombs of the Early Bronze Age were multiple burials,

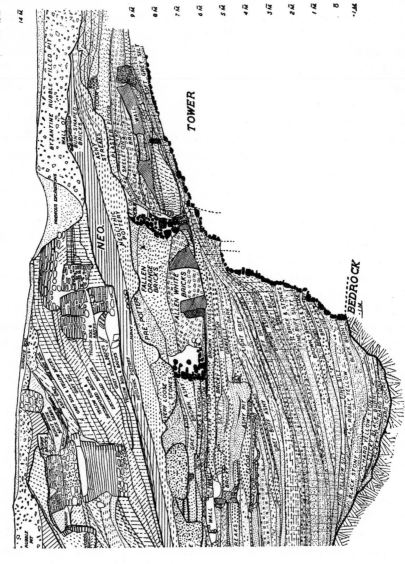

FIG. 2. Part of section of Trench I at Jericho, showing, upper left and centre, succession of Early Bronze Age town walls, overlain, upper left, by E.B.–M.B. house and upper part of Middle Bronze Age rampart.

with at Jericho up to 100 individuals, with a process of piling
skeletalized remains and discarding many of the bones (e.g.

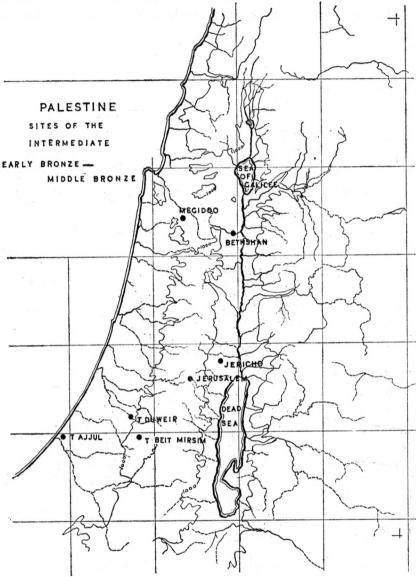

PALESTINE

SITES OF THE

INTERMEDIATE

EARLY BRONZE —

MIDDLE BRONZE

MEGIDDO

BETHSHAN

SEA
OF
GALILEE

JERICHO

JERUSALEM

DEAD
SEA

T DUWEIR

T AJJUL

T BEIT MIRSIM

FIG. 3. Sites providing evidence of the Intermediate Early Bronze–Middle Bronze
period in Palestine.

Fig. 4). The E.B.–M.B. burials were essentially of single individuals to a tomb, and this distinction is found everywhere,
with again the exception of Megiddo.

The pottery is so distinct that even if only small sherds are
found it is usually quite possible to be certain as to the attribu-

tion. The particular characteristic of the E.B.–M.B. pottery is the gritty, sandy texture and the thinness of the ware, and there is the strange practice that the body of the vessel is hand-made, usually with pronounced finger-marks in the interior, while the

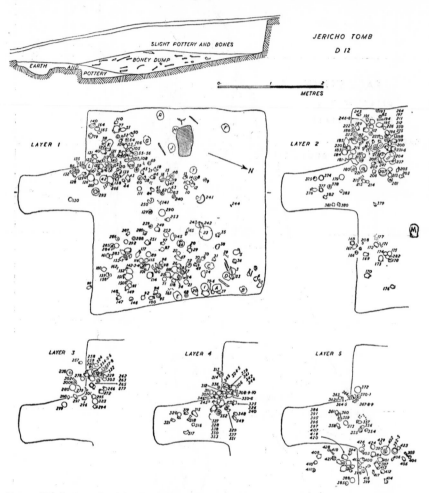

FIG. 4. Typical tomb of the Early Bronze Age at Jericho with piled skulls and offerings and very few long bones.

rim is made on a fast wheel. In colour it is drab or greenish, and in most groups without any coloured slip or burnish, in very obvious contrast with the red burnished slip that is so common in the Early Bronze Age and reappears in the Middle Bronze Age.

Copper or bronze weapons of any sort are comparatively rare in Early Bronze Age Palestine. In the E.B.–M.B. period they become very common; in particular daggers are of very frequent occurrence in the graves of some groups. The distinction in the form of the weapons of this period can be seen in

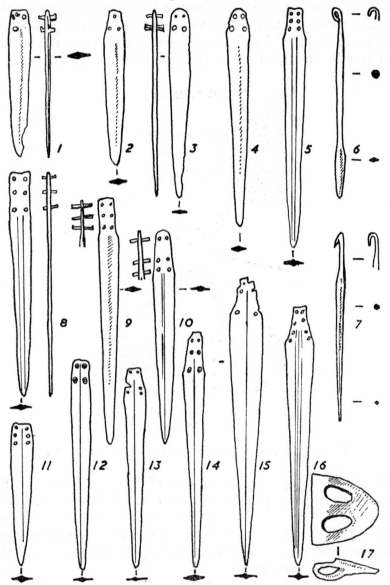

FIG. 5. Weapons of the E.B.–M.B. period from Jericho (1–10), T. Ajjul (11–16), and Megiddo (17). ⅕

a comparison of Fig. 5 with Fig. 26 and Pl. II. 1, illustrating weapons of the Middle Bronze Age.

This comparison of features of the E.B.–M.B. period with those of the preceding period has already emphasized some of its characteristics. The evidence is clear that newcomers destroyed the urban civilization of the Early Bronze Age, and substituted something entirely different, in which walled towns played no part. Incidental reference has been made to another characteristic, in the allusion to groups among the population. The excavation of Jericho first drew attention to this aspect, and it will be necessary to describe the Jericho evidence in

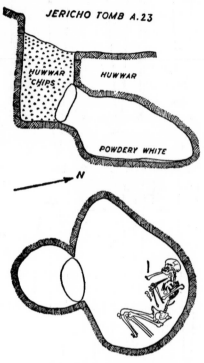

Fig. 6. Typical tomb of the Jericho E.B.–M.B. Dagger type.

some detail to support the validity of this argument that the recognition of these groups is important. Of the 507 tombs excavated, 346 were first used in this period. Within this number, evidence of the practice of seven quite distinct burial customs could be observed, to which names emphasizing the particular characteristics were given.

The simplest type, with 105 examples, was the Dagger type.[1] In these the shaft was shallow, small (with a diameter *c.* 1 m.), and noticeably neatly cut (Pl. II. 2, Fig. 6). The chamber was likewise small, with an average diameter of 1.50 m. In this small chamber, a single individual, or occasionally two, was placed carefully in a crouched position (Pl. I. 2). The name was

[1] *Jericho I*, pp. 186–99; *Jericho II*, pp. 50–57.

given to this class since the typical offering was a dagger, placed beside the body in such a way as to suggest it was in a shoulder sling or at the waist as it had been worn by its owner.[1] The type of dagger is stereotyped, and is similar to that found in other burials of the period in which daggers are found (Fig. 5). Those individuals not provided with daggers were probably women, and for them a pin or some beads represent the only grave goods. In no case were any pottery vessels found in tombs of this type. The impression given is of a group of people of austere habits, possessing little in the way of worldly goods, amongst whom a warrior element was very important.

This type of burial is linked to the second and most numerous type, the Pottery type (161 examples), only by the practice of single burials, or again occasionally two, in each tomb. The size of the shaft is much greater, with an average width of 2 m. and depth of 3 m., and the shaft is much more roughly cut (Pl. III. 1). The entrance to the chamber at the base of the shaft is no larger than in the case of the Dagger type, a bare minimum through which to pull a body, but the chamber is much larger, typically an elongated rectangle c. 2·75 m. by 2·50 m., though with its height only c. 1·10 m. (Fig. 7). This comparatively large chamber contained the burial of an individual (Pl. III. 2) with his grave goods, a group of little pottery vessels (Pl. IV. 1, fig. 8), of a type that seems to be either purely funerary, or, alternatively, to show that this group, burying on the outskirts of the ancient town of Jericho, did not actually live there, for the pottery on the tell of this period is of different forms, though similar technique. No weapons at all were found in burials of this type. Another difference is that in nearly all the Pottery type tombs, but none of those of the Dagger type, a lamp, of the square four-nozzle form characteristic of the period, was placed in a niche cut in the wall of the chamber. Not only were the Dagger type and the Pottery type differentiated by the grave goods, but the treatment of the bodies was markedly different. The bodies of the individuals placed in the Pottery type tomb were all decomposed to a greater or lesser extent. In some the bones were completely disordered, and must have been deposited in the chamber as a collection of bones in a container. In other instances parts of the skeleton were in articulation, and decomposition was therefore not so far advanced when the body was deposited, though usually far enough for there to be an appreciable displacement of limbs. This practice of providing large

[1] *Jericho II*, pp. 553–5.

and deeply excavated tombs for a collection of disordered bones does not seem to be accounted for by the length of time needed to

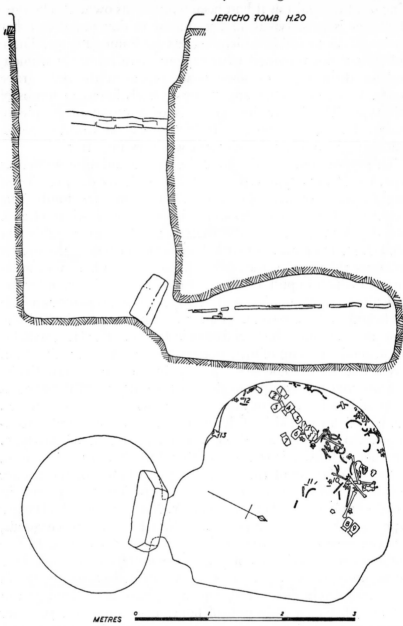

Fɪɢ. 7. Typical tomb of the Jericho E.B.–M.B. Pottery type.

prepare the tomb chamber, for there is evidence for a lapse of time between the cutting of the tomb and the burial,[1] and other

[1] *Jericho I*, pp. 217–19.

evidence suggests that the tombs were not prepared by those who were buried in them,[1] but rather by professional tomb-

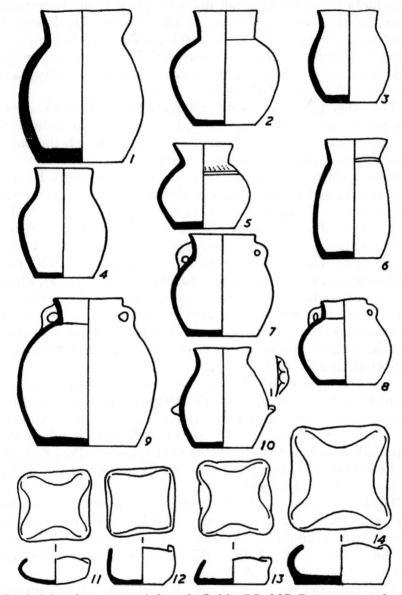

FIG. 8. Selected pottery vessels from the Jericho E.B.–M.B. Pottery type tombs. $\frac{1}{5}$

diggers who had them ready at hand as required. The probable explanation for the burial of decomposed bodies is that the group that buried in this way were nomadic pastoralists. Before entry into Palestine, they may have followed a seasonal

[1] *Jericho II*, pp. 551–3.

pattern of migration, returning at intervals to an ancestral burying ground, and bringing with them the bodies of those who had died in the interval, many of which would necessarily have suffered decomposition in the process. In Palestine, seasonal movements with flocks and herds may well have ranged from the Jordan Valley in the winter to the hill-country in the summer, and Jericho, perhaps as the first point of entry, may have served as the tribal centre.

The other groups of tombs differentiated by burial customs are not so important numerically, but have equally individual characteristics. The most striking are those to which the name Outsize was given (thirty-four examples). Though still intended only for a single body, in size they far exceed that of the Pottery type tombs, with shafts averaging 4·35 m. deep, and an extreme example 7 m. deep, and chamber up to 5·90 by 4 m., and a height of *c*. 1·80 m. (Fig. 9). The shafts are not only wide, but are rectangular in plan, in contrast to the round plan of the other types. The finds are equally on a large scale. The pots are numerous, and mainly large and fat (Fig. 10, Pl. IV. 2), which distinguishes them from the tooth-brush-mug-like vessels of the Pottery type tombs, and another distinguishing feature is that a number of vessels have spouts (Pl. IV. 2). As well as pottery vessels, weapons are found in these tombs, and also numerous copper studs and bindings.

A fourth type, of which there were only five examples, was named the Square-shaft type. This shape is thus like that of the Outsize type tombs, but the size was very much smaller, and the distribution was different. In size of shaft and chamber, this type falls between those of the Dagger type and Pottery type, and the finds include both vessels and weapons, a combination never found in those tombs.

The fifth type is marked by a great poverty of finds, only copper pins and studs, and beads, from which it was called the Bead type (thirty examples). The chambers were rather small and ill cut, and the shafts shallow, the resultant thinness of the roof having often caused a collapse.

All these types have such distinctive features, not only in one but in a number of characteristics, that there seems no ground to suppose that one emerged out of another. There is also little ground for ascribing the differences to a chronological succession. One Pottery type tomb cut into a Dagger tomb, but the main concentrations of the individual types are distinct (Fig. 11), and where they overlap, the tomb-diggers have been sufficiently aware of the existence of the other tombs to avoid them, except in this one instance. It might possibly be suggested that the Outsize type tombs come late, since they are concentrated

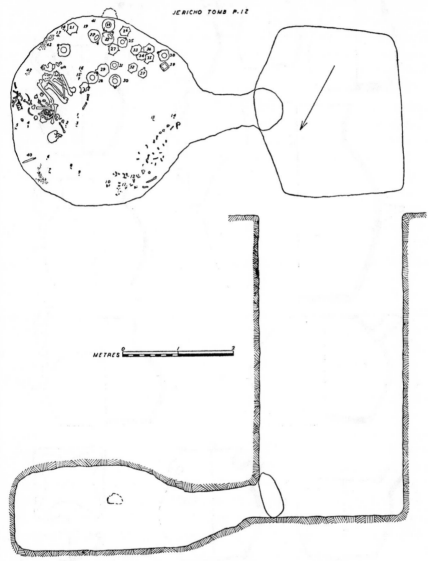

JERICHO TOMB P.12

METRES

FIG. 9. Typical tomb of the Jericho E.B.–M.B. Outsize type.

in an area on the outskirts of the main cemetery, but this and the one case of overlap are insufficient grounds to support a theory of succession.

The characteristics of the sixth type of tomb, the Composite type (10 examples), could, however, be interpreted as combining those of all the five already mentioned. Both pottery and

weapons are found, and the pottery vessels are sometimes those
of the Pottery type tombs and sometimes of the Outsize tombs.

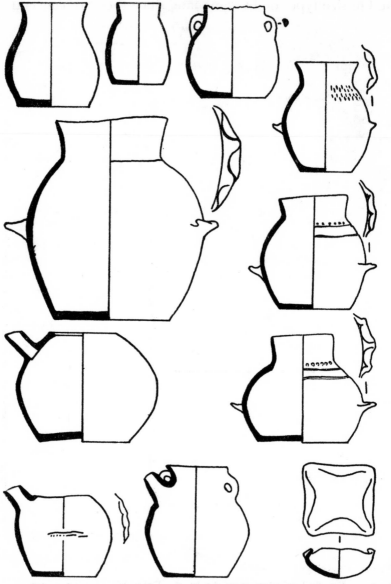

FIG. 10. Selected pottery vessels from the Jericho E.B.–M.B. Outsize type tombs. $\frac{1}{5}$

The form and size of the shafts and chambers have some of
the characteristics of the other types, though they do not
approach the size of the Outsize type. The distribution of these
Composite type tombs is fairly widespread. These features may
therefore suggest that these tombs represent a secondary period
in which there is some mingling of population.

Of the final type, the Multiple-burial type, there is only one example, which might be thought to be insufficient to constitute a separate type. But its difference from the other tombs

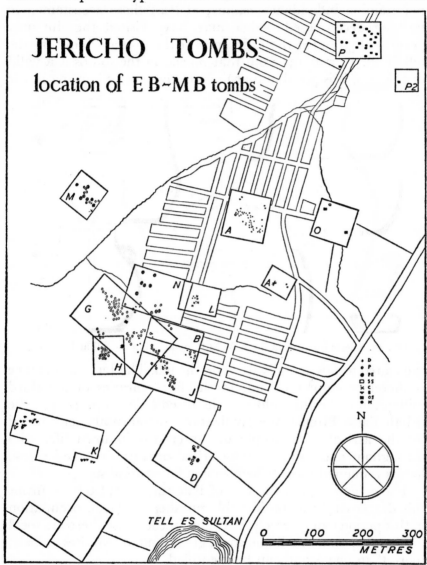

FIG. 11. Distribution of the different types of E.B.–M.B. tombs at Jericho.

lies not only in the fact that it contained three bodies, but also in a quite distinctive group of pottery vessels, including cups and dishes, noticeably missing from the 345 other tombs. This pottery is of particular interest, since it alone is really close to that from southern sites such as T. Ajjul.[1]

[1] The pottery forms are analysed in *Jericho II*, pp. 38–47.

The most probable explanation of this evidence of varying burial practices is that they represent the habits of separate tribal groups, alike using Jericho as a centre; but otherwise maintaining individual customs; at least those accustomed to burying decomposed bodies may have visited the site only periodically, and if the difference of the pottery found on the tell (Figs. 12 and 13) from that placed in the tombs is a valid distinction, it is possible that none of the groups burying in the

FIG. 12. Selected pottery of the E.B.–M.B. period from the tell at Jericho. ⅕

excavated tombs actually lived on the tell. The Jericho evidence is therefore emphatic that, in the last centuries of the third millennium (the chronology is discussed below, pp. 33–35), the urban Early Bronze Age civilization was abruptly terminated by the arrival of a people not interested in town life, who throughout maintained a loose tribal organization, and whose habits remained those of semi-nomadic pastoralists.

The evidence from the rest of Palestine completely confirms this diagnosis. In a considerable number of places, occupation of this period can be recognized. But in each case there are local differences, some small and some great, and at two sites at least, more than one group can be identified.

The first of these is T. Ajjul. There, Sir Flinders Petrie excavated two cemeteries, separately located, the 100–200 Cemetery and the 1500 Cemetery.[1] It is probable that, as at Jericho, the users of these cemeteries did not have a town or even village centre, as no remains attributable to them have been recorded on the great Middle Bronze Age town site, though

[1] *Ancient Gaza II.*

the excavation of the lower levels was too incomplete for this
to be certain. The two cemeteries have their differing characteristics, in some ways allied to those of Jericho, but quite
definitely not identical. In the 1500 Cemetery, the shafts were in
plan rectangular, thus resembling the Square-shaft type at
Jericho; the burials in the chambers were, with very few excep-

FIG. 13. Selected pottery of the E.B.–M.B. period from the tell at Jericho. $\frac{1}{10}$

tions, of intact bodies in a crouched position, thus resembling
those in the Jericho Dagger type tombs; over a third of these
tombs contained a dagger (Fig. 5. 11–16), near to but not
identical with those in the Jericho tombs, in some cases as the
sole offering, but in contrast to the Jericho Dagger type tombs,
some also had pottery vessels, tall, flat-based jars with flaring
rims and very vestigial ledge handles (Fig. 14. 4–6), a type in
the Jericho tombs only related to the single Multiple-burial
tomb. In the 100–200 Cemetery, the shafts are in plan approximately circular; the burials are of disarticulated skeletons,[1] thus
resembling those in especially the Pottery type tombs at Jericho,
but also in all others except the Dagger type tombs; only two

[1] *ADAJ* iii, p. 42.

tombs of the whole group have daggers, but two have javelins, found at Jericho in the Square-shaft and Composite type tombs,

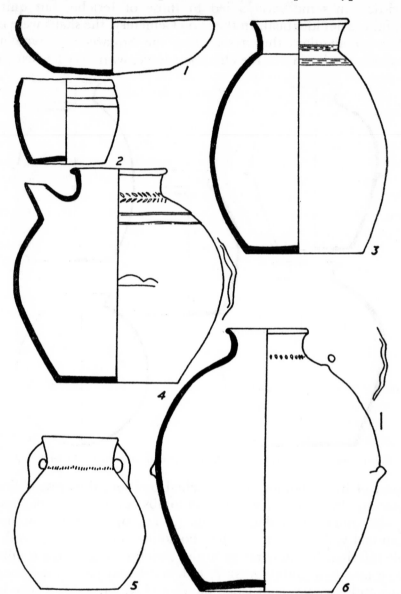

FIG. 14. Selected pottery from T. Ajjul cemetery 100–200 (1–3) and cemetery 1500 (4–6). $\frac{1}{8}$

but never in the Pottery type tombs; the pottery vessels (Fig. 14. 1–3) are mainly jars, which never have the vestigial ledge handles almost universal in the 1500 Cemetery, and there are also some dishes and bowls, not found in the 1500 Cemetery, and only found at Jericho in the Multiple-burial type tomb. These two cemeteries at T. Ajjul are again best explained as evidence of two separate groups. The only suggestion of typological development, that jars with vestigial ledge handles are earlier than jars in which no vestiges of handles survive, is not sufficient to counterbalance the other different features for which no typological sequence can be suggested.

Other sites in southern Palestine are linked with T. Ajjul by the predominance of tall, flat-based jars with flaring rims. But in no case are the jars quite identical with those of T. Ajjul. At T. Duweir, the jars (Figs. 15 and 16) tend to be taller and narrower, and to have knob or lug handles; the tombs here are of a variety of forms which do not seem to go with any other particular set of characteristics; some tombs have daggers, and a few have javelins. At T. Beit Mirsim another slightly divergent type of flaring-rim jar was found, but no tombs were located, and, perhaps as a consequence, no weapons found. As has already been said (p. 9) at neither of these sites was there any real town occupation.

Over the rest of the hill-country of southern and central Palestine there is a scatter of finds recorded which can be attributed to this period, almost all of it from tombs. Much of the pottery resembles that from the southern sites, but in the neighbourhood of Jerusalem tomb groups have been found, unfortunately of ill-defined provenance, with vessels resembling those from the Jericho Pottery type tombs.

In northern Palestine there is clearly a different influence. Similarity of pottery technique and the occurrence of some vessels, especially the little lug-handled jars (e.g. Figs. 8. 7–9, 10. 3, 12. 7, 14. 5, 15. 3, 18. 10, 19. 4) and the four-nozzle lamps found in all groups makes it clear that the finds belong to the same period. The closest links are with the Outsize type tombs at Jericho, but neither the vessels nor the burial customs are identical.

The most important site is Megiddo, where again there appear to be two groups. The most interesting of these is the people burying in the tombs to which the excavators of Megiddo gave the name of Shaft Tombs. This name at Jericho would be undiagnostic, for all the tombs have, or originally had, rock-cut chambers approached by shafts. At Megiddo it so happened that the great majority of burials were found on the tell, as graves or built tombs in the accumulated soil. Only in the clearance of areas for dumping on the slopes below the tell to the south-east were rock-cut tombs of this type found. But though the name is not distinctive, the type of tomb is. It was

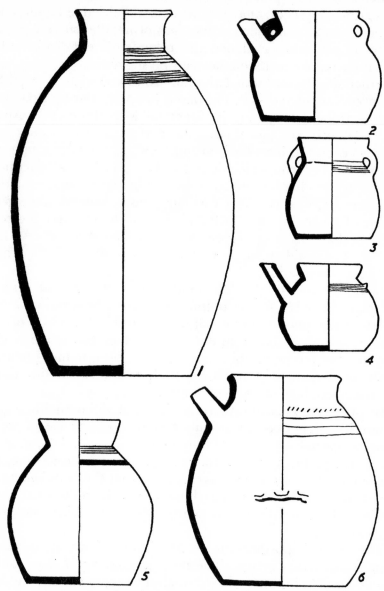

FIG. 15. Selected pottery from T. Duweir E.B.–M.B. tombs. ⅛

almost rigidly stereotyped, with a rectangular shaft from which there was access to one end of a central chamber, on the three other sides of which were side chambers at a slightly higher level, all approximately rectangular (Fig. 17). This elaborate form of tomb is not paralleled in Palestine until the last centuries B.C.

Many of these tombs had been re-used at later periods. But where they were intact, the burial customs were uniform. The skeletons seem in many cases to be of disarticulated skeletons. This was not recognized by the excavators, for the idea of burying skeletalized remains did not become an obvious interpretation until clear evidence of this was found at Jericho, but this is the only possible explanation of the carefully recorded facts of the condition of the skeletons. In this respect, the burials in the

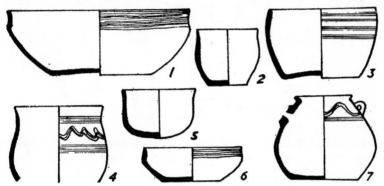

FIG. 16. Selected pottery from T. Duweir E.B.–M.B. tombs. ⅕

Shaft Tombs resemble some of those at Jericho, especially the Pottery type tombs, but in every other respect they are different.

There is in the first place the plan of the tombs. Secondly, the tombs are obviously designed to contain multiple burials, and, where the evidence is complete enough to form deductions, it can be seen that they did in fact do so. Thirdly, the range of pottery is different (Fig. 18). There are connexions with other sites; the little lug-handled jar (Fig. 18. 10) may be compared with Fig. 8. 7 from Jericho and Fig. 15. 3 from T. Duweir; the jar (Fig. 18. 1) with its folded ledge handles may be compared with several jars from Jericho Outsize type tombs,[1] and Fig. 18. 4, similarly with Fig. 10, centre bottom, from the Jericho Outsize type tombs. But in addition to these vessels that are perfectly at home in the E.B.–M.B. groups of Palestine, there are a number of others that are alien. The most striking difference is that they are completely wheel-made. They include the goblet (Fig. 18. 9), unique at Megiddo, strap-handled jugs, e.g. Fig. 18. 7–8, and the 'tea-pots' (Fig. 18. 2–3), wide-mouthed jars with spouts, decorated in dark paint on a light ground; to

[1] e.g. from Jericho Tomb P. 22, *Jericho II*, fig. 53. 9, and Tomb P. 24, *ibid*. fig. 68. 2.

these last, other vessels in the usual Palestinian technique and in the usual drab finish are clearly related, and may be local copies.

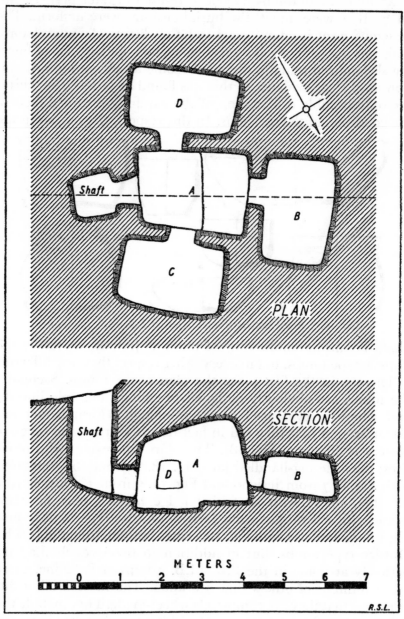

FIG. 17. Typical plan and section of Shaft Tomb at Megiddo.

These alien vessels provide a key to the origins of these newcomers in Palestine. They are clearly related to those found in Syria, for instance at Qatna (Fig. 23) and T. 'As (Fig. 24), sites to be discussed below. Equally important are the metal objects, especially pins (Pl. V. 1). These can be paralleled on a large num-

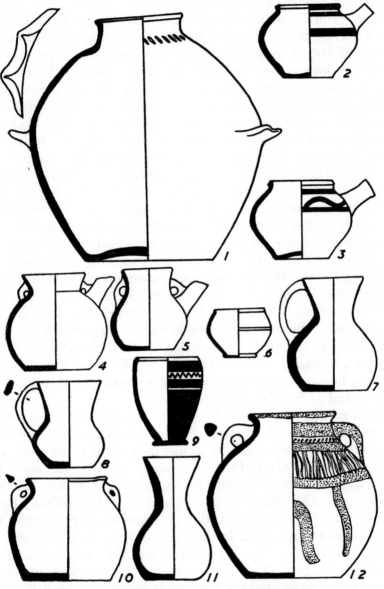

FIG. 18. Selected pottery from Megiddo Shaft Tombs. ⅕

ber of Syrian sites, for instance in Tomb I at Tell 'As (Fig. 24),[1] at Byblos,[2] and as far afield as Tell Brak in the Khabur.[3] Though comparable tomb types have not yet been found in Syria, there

[1] *Syria*, xiii, pl. xxxix.    [2] *Byblos I*, pl. lxix.
[3] *Iraq*, ix, pl. xxxi.

can be no doubt that the group that buried its dead in these tombs had a fairly immediate origin in Syria, or at least that there was a close common ancestor.

The second group at Megiddo, Tombs 1101–2 B Lower, did not excavate these elaborate tombs. The burials are found in a series of rough interconnecting rock-cut chambers, entered from the slope of the tell. The chambers were used for occupation during the Proto-Urban and Early Bronze periods and above the occupation layers are burials.[1] In them could be identified the remains of fourteen individuals. The skeletons are described by the excavators as disturbed, but it is clear from present evidence that again the bodies were largely decomposed before burial took place. The pottery (Fig. 19) has its links with that of the Shaft Tombs, with the little lug-handled jar again appearing, but with notable differences, especially the less flatly folded ledge-handles and the round-bottom jars, and the absence of the imported jugs, vases, and tea-pots and the local copies of the latter. The pottery therefore has less obvious links with Syria, though the general character is not dissimilar; on the other hand, in the metal objects (Pl. V. 2), there is a very important link. These include, with spearheads that can be paralleled at Byblos, a swollen-headed toggle pin which is a type fossil of the period, occurring at Ras Shamra (Pl. V. 3, Fig. 22), Byblos (Pls. X, XIII, XX. 1), Tell 'As (Fig. 24), and many other sites. Associated with these objects is a dagger of the type found at Jericho and T. Ajjul.

Both groups of tombs at Megiddo are unlike those previously discussed alike in their form and their contents. It is probable that the occupation was also unlike that of the other sites. The stratification of Megiddo is not easy to disentangle, since the excavation was in schematic strata, unrelated to actual levels. Buildings can be related to pottery and to periods only by probability, in which the recognition of terracing of the slope of the mound must play a part. In the levels ascribed by the excavators to the Early Bronze Age is a group of temples. An analysis of the evidence[2] suggests that they represent three successive stages. The temple of the final stage certainly belongs to the E.B.–M.B. period, for incorporated in its walls was a fenestrated axehead (cf. Fig. 5. 17) of a type certainly belonging to this period,[3] being

---

[1] The occupation layers and burial layers are confused in the publication in *Megiddo Tombs*, pp. 24–27, but an analysis makes the distinction quite clear.    [2] Kenyon, *Eretz Israel*, v, pp. 55*–60*.

[3] Kenyon, 'A Crescentic Axehead from Jericho, and a group of weapons

found in a Shaft Tomb at Megiddo[1] and on the tell at Jericho,[2] as well as in great numbers at Byblos.[3] This final temple at

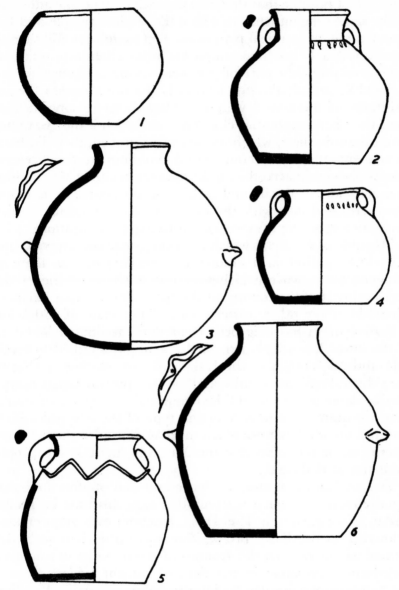

FIG. 19. Selected pottery from Megiddo Tombs 1101–2 B Lower. ⅕

from Tell el Hesi', *Eleventh Annual Report of the Institute of Archaeology, University of London*, pp. 1–9.

[1] *Megiddo Tombs*, pl. 163. 8.

[2] *Jericho 1907–1909*, fig. 105. Found with a collection of flat copper celts (cf. Byblos) in an E.B.–M.B. lug-handled jar, *ibid.*, pl. 22. 29.

[3] *Byblos I*, pl. LXV; *Byblos II*, pl. LX, pl. LXIII, pl. LXXVIII &c.

Megiddo differs from its predecessors in that the centre of the structure has been filled in to make a much smaller cella, but it is at least possible that this is an alteration by people adhering to the same religious cult, to whom the original temple and the twin temples of identical plan of the first stage were still sacred. But even if only the final temple stage, together with adjacent structures probably part of the same layout, belongs to the E.B.–M.B. period, the implication is that at Megiddo the inhabitants of the period were considerably more sophisticated than their contemporaries elsewhere, and even if they were not true urban dwellers, which has yet to be proved, they did have permanent and even monumental buildings at their centre. This is perhaps in accord with the character of the Shaft Tombs, so much more elaborate and architectural than anything found elsewhere, and also with the evidence of closer contacts with Syria, nearer to the Mesopotamian centre of civilization.

Megiddo is the site at which the evidence of this aspect of the E.B.–M.B. period in Palestine is best known, but there is evidence from two other sites that it is characteristic of the northern part of the country at the time. The site that balances Megiddo at the other, eastern, end of the Plain of Esdraelon is Beth-shan. It has long been clear that the limited sounding of the lower levels included, in the material ascribed to levels XII and XI, pottery of the E.B.–M.B. period close to that of the Megiddo Shaft Tombs and of the Jericho Outsize type tombs. Among the unpublished material[1] are plans of tombs that are quite undoubtedly of the type of the Megiddo Shaft Tombs, though they were much mutilated in subsequent re-use. There can be no doubt that the Megiddo Shaft Tomb people were also at Beth-shan.

There is, on the pottery evidence and that of other finds, an equally close connexion with another site, this time in Transjordan.[2] In a cave near T. el Husn, a deposit overlying remains belonging to the Early Bronze Age was rather hesitantly described as funerary on the grounds of the presence of fragmentary human remains; in the light of present evidence, these fragmentary remains can be interpreted as skeletalized bodies. The great mass of material in this deposit consisted of pottery very recognizably connected with that from the Shaft Tombs

[1] Prepared for publication by Mr. G. M. Fitzgerald, and kindly made available by the author and the Philadelphia University Museum through the agency of Mrs. Garner James.

[2] *APEF* vi, G. Lankester Harding, 'Four Tomb Groups from Jordan'.

of Megiddo, with the same range of forms, and the occasional vessel decorated in bands and streaks of paint; another similarity is the occurrence of two pins with curled heads that also occur in these tombs (cf. Pl. V. 1). A branch of the people who penetrated into the Plain of Esdraelon thus must have established themselves east of the Jordan.

The Palestinian evidence has been described in detail, for, as has already been said, here only is detail available. Whatever nomenclature is given to the period (see above, p. 8), the cultural sequence is clear. Between the urban civilization of the Early Bronze Age and the urban civilization of the Middle Bronze Age there is an interlude, for which the evidence comes from tombs and not from settlements, the evidence that is to say of a numerous but nomadic (or at least semi-nomadic) population. Varying interpretations have been suggested for the differences between the groups that have been described, mainly based on a typological succession of ceramic features and therefore a chronological succession of groups, but it is here suggested that the differences between them cannot be explained in this way, since for many of the contrasting features there is no typological succession. It is therefore here claimed that the differences are accounted for as characteristics of allied but distinct contemporary groups. The emphasis is thus on a tribal organization, and many other features suggest a semi-nomadic way of life, that of warriors and pastoralists, in accord with this interpretation.

So far, only the evidence of the area west of the Jordan has been discussed, with the exception of that from El Husn. In Transjordan generally, the area subsequently known as Moab and Gilead, and for the Negeb, there is evidence that there was considerable occupation at this period. But since it seems probable that there was a difference in subsequent history, without the same demarcation in these areas between this period and the next, this problem is discussed below (p. 64).

The chronology of the period is a matter of inference. Seminomadic pastoralists are apt at all periods to be non-literate, and Palestine was at that time a fringe area between the literate civilizations of Mesopotamia and Egypt. From contacts with Egypt we can only say that Early Bronze III overlapped the time of the IVth Dynasty of Egypt (2600–2500 B.C.) and that the Middle Bronze Age begins during the time of the XIIth Dynasty (1991–1786 B.C.). Within this time is the period of the First Intermediate of Egypt, starting with the fall of the VIth

Dynasty (c. 2185 B.C.), after which time Egypt no longer sent trading parties to Syria to bring back cedar wood, and other products,[1] and ending only effectively with the rise of the XIIth Dynasty. This collapse of ordered government in Egypt was due to incursions of Asiatics, and a prelude to such disorders is to be expected in Palestine. But the genesis of this period of Asiatic disturbances long precedes the fall of the VIth Egyptian Dynasty, for its centre was geographically far distant. As early as the time of Sargon of Akkad (2371–2316 B.C.) the Amurru begin to appear in the Mesopotamian record. At first there was probably peaceful infiltration, but by the time of the IIIrd Dynasty of Ur (2113–2004 B.C.) warlike threats had become frequent. All the references show that these people came to Mesopotamia from the west. They can be recognized as nomads or semi-nomads; Ibbi-Sin of Ur, for instance, calls them vagabonds who have never known what a town was. This is then the setting of the Intermediate Early Bronze–Middle Bronze period in Palestine, that of disturbances seriously affecting the great Empires of the Tigris–Euphrates and Nile valleys caused by the movement of nomads, who, at least in the north, are identified as Amurru. The area of much weaker political powers in Syria and Palestine would be all the more disastrously affected. Since we know that the nomads in the north were Amorites, and since the connexion between groups in Syria and Palestine can be shown (to be discussed more fully below) we have here the interpretation of the archaeological evidence; the Amorites of the Bible were emerging.

The scanty direct archaeological evidence for chronology agrees in placing the E.B.–M.B. of Palestine in this period. The links between the pottery of the Megiddo Shaft Tombs with Syrian sites has already been mentioned. At Qatna, these types (Fig. 23) are found on the *butte de l'Église* beneath a temple ascribed to Ninegal, and dated to c. 2200 B.C. A group of pins found with very similar material at Tell 'As (Fig. 24) is paralleled in the same tombs, and is, moreover, paralleled at Brak, where Professor Mallowan dates these likewise to c. 2200 B.C. The links between Syria and the southern sites in Palestine are not quite so striking, but the peculiar decoration of pottery vessels with incised or combed wavy lines, found for instance at T. Beit Mirsim, T. Duweir, and Jericho, is very closely paralleled at Ras Shamra (Fig. 22). It is probable that the period of the dominance of the nomads would be longer in Palestine than

[1] *CAH*, vol. i, ch. xxi, § i.

in the area of stronger powers, and the evidence concerning both the Early Bronze Age and the Middle Bronze Age would tend to curtail rather than stretch their chronological limits, so a range *c.* 2300 B.C. to 1900 B.C. could well be given to the E.B.–M.B. period.

# II

# THE INTERMEDIATE EARLY BRONZE–MIDDLE BRONZE PERIOD IN SYRIA

THIS nomenclature has not hitherto been used by archaeologists working in Syria. For the most part it has not been identified as a separate cultural phase, for there is a sad lack of evidence for stratigraphic succession in Syria. M. Schaeffer at Ras Shamra did, however, recognize the very distinctive features that appear, and he very strikingly associates them with the arrival of a new people by giving to them the name *porteurs de torques*. The period he designates Middle Ugarit I, but no more than in Palestine is there any evidence of connexion with the succeeding full Middle Bronze Age. The term Intermediate Early Bronze–Middle Bronze is as applicable in Syria as in Palestine, and is here used to emphasize the links between the two areas.

Ras Shamra (Pl. VI. 1) is the imposing site in northern coastal Syria which is shown from the epigraphic material found there to have been Ugarit and the capital of a wealthy state. Its position in the fertile coastal plain, with its port of Minet el Beida only a kilometre away, gave it a natural wealth and the opportunities of foreign trade. It is not surprising that excavations have shown that its history is a long one, with origins in the Neolithic. At its maximum extent the site was large, with massive ramparts enclosing a trapezoidal area of c. 47 acres. The period of greatest importance of Ras Shamra, to which most of the remains recovered belong, was the Middle and Late Bronze Ages, covering the greater part of the second millennium B.C. It seems probable that it is only to these periods that the maximum expansion of the city belongs. Within the comparatively level area enclosed by the ramparts, there is a higher area in the north-western corner; its outline does not show well in the air photographs, for it is obscured by the long lines of excavation dumps, but the difference between the upper and lower levels can be seen in Pl. VI. 2, and the outlines are shown in the contoured plan (Fig. 20). This area Schaeffer in his earlier reports[1] calls the acropolis, but in the later ones[2] the upper town, and this seems the better description. As far

[1] *Syria*, x, xii–xvi.  [2] *Syria*, xviii–xx.

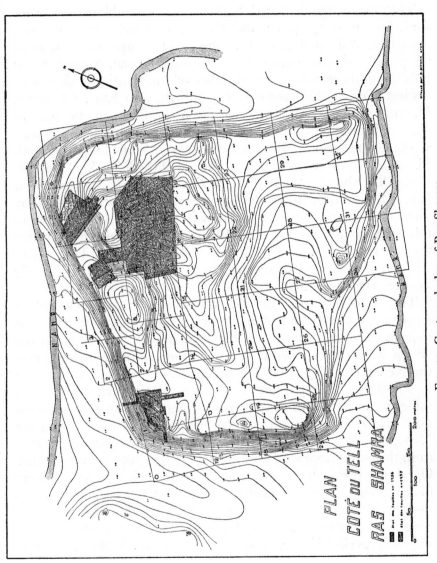

Fig. 20. Contoured plan of Ras Shamra.

as evidence is at present available, it is here suggested that this was the site of the early settlement, and was the original tell, for it was, as will be suggested below, not until a date well into the Middle Bronze Age that there was the great expansion to the area enclosed by the ramparts.

This suggestion is based both on the resemblance to other sites, for instance Qatna and Hazor, at which there was this sequence, and on the fact that the early occupation was, as so far published, concentrated in this higher area. Schaeffer has published three schematic sections of the stratigraphical succession (*Stratigraphie comparée*, Pls. v, viii, and xiii). Of these, Pl. xiii represents the evidence for a sounding in the part of what will here be called the original tell, while both Pls. v and viii show soundings in the northern quarter at the foot of this tell. Pl. viii shows no remains below a burial of the E.B.–M.B. period, while Pl. v shows a single sherd of Tell Halaf ware just below an E.B.–M.B. burial, from which it must be separated in time by some two thousand years. It is clear therefore that at least in this area outside the limits of the original tell, the first effective use was as a burial area in the E.B.–M.B. period, and that there was no occupation until the time of the overlying Middle Bronze Age houses.

The objects shown on Pl. xiii represent a much longer sequence, though one which can be by no means complete. The objects shown at the base of the drawing do not represent the lowest levels, for subsequent excavations continued down into the Neolithic. The published material[1] begins with a group of sherds of the El Ubeid–Jemdat Nasr period covering the fourth millennium B.C. This pottery would suggest that at this period northern Syria as far as the Mediterranean coast fell within the Mesopotamian sphere of influence, and differentiates the area from the contemporary Palestine, where this pottery is not found. Overlying these levels is a deposit *c*. 3 m. thick in which were found many sherds of unidentified coarse pottery. Such a deposit, with many sherds, suggests that the site was occupied. Since the contemporary, and well-known, wares of the Early Dynastic period in Mesopotamia and the Early Bronze Age in

---

[1] It should be noted that the section appears to represent a composite illustration of evidence for different sites. Most of the early group of sherds are published in *Syria*, xvi, but nos. 54 and 60 come from a cut published in *Syria*, xv, on the northern slope of the original tell. Moreover, it would seem from *Syria*, xvi, p. 160, that the Early Bronze Age group did not come from the same cut as the earlier group.

Palestine were not observed, and no structures are recorded, it seems likely to be a period of retrogressive culture, perhaps derived from an indigenous Chalcolithic, of which the evidence of structural remains was so slight that it escaped observation. Occupation there must have been, to build up this 3 m. of deposit, and the fire with which it ended is again proof of a preceding occupation with structures that could be burnt.

Dug into this fill were deposits, some at least apparently graves, containing pottery of which the published vessels[1] are clearly related to the Early Bronze Age III of Palestine; two are bowls of Khirbet Kerak ware,[2] and the jars with their combed decoration can be compared with those found in T. Beit Mirsim Stratum J.[3] The possibility that this period, about the middle of the third millennium B.C., is one at which there was a major contribution to the culture of the Mediterranean coastal area is very interesting, but its consideration is outside the scope of the present study. As far as Ras Shamra is concerned, a considerably wider examination of the levels of the period is required.

The constant feature of the next stage at Ras Shamra is the appearance of the material ascribed by Schaeffer to a people he graphically calls the *porteurs de torques*.[4] He uses this name since among the objects found, and also worn by figurines attributed to this period, was a type of torc characterized by curled ends (Fig. 21. 50).[5] The other characteristic finds were swollen-headed or club-headed toggle pins, triangular-bladed daggers, heavy bracelets, socketed spearheads, fenestrated axeheads, biconical beads (Fig. 22), and ornaments in the form of watch-spring-like spirals (Fig. 21. 52).

It would appear that almost all the finds of the period came from burials. It is not in fact clear that any of them came from occupation levels. The material illustrated in *Stratigraphie comparée*, Pl. XIII, came from burials in the original tell, but it has not been published as separate groups. It includes two pottery vessels (fig. 22. 5, 11), which apparently, with another bowl, formed a separate group together with a mushroom-headed pin and a socketed spearhead. The decoration of the two-handled cup, in wavy combed lines between straight lines, is clearly related to that form in E.B.–M.B. deposits in Palestine (cf.

---

[1] *Stratigraphie comparée*, pl. XIII, 46–50; *Ugaritica II*, fig. 99. 7–14.
[2] Cf. e.g. *Beth-shan*, pl. VIII. 9, and *Jericho I*, fig. 38. 29–35.
[3] *AASOR* xiii, pl. I. 1–2.
[4] *Ugaritica II*, pp. 49–120.
[5] Only two are in fact illustrated.

Figs. 12. 3–4 and 16. 4). These are the only pottery vessels published. Other burials, some apparently with intact crouched skeletons, had the other objects shown on Fig. 22, but which objects were associated together is indicated only in a very few cases.[1] At the foot of the tell, other burials were found of which the finds from two are illustrated as groups[2] (Pl. V. 3). Both these burials include ornaments from the list given above, and it is not clear if burials with weapons were found in this area.

It is to be hoped that subsequent publications of the Ras Shamra material will give a fuller catalogue of the contents of

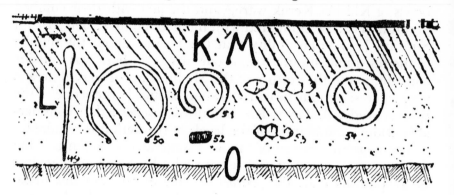

FIG. 21. E.B.–M.B. burial group from Ras Shamra.

individual graves, for it is clear that the finds of this period aroused M. Schaeffer's interest. This would make it possible to see whether at Ras Shamra there was any of the evidence for separate groups that is shown by the contemporary tombs in Palestine. It might be hazarded that the suggestion that only with a single burial was there pottery might be a pointer in this direction.

At any rate, the evidence from Ras Shamra suggests a stage comparable with that of Palestine. Dug into a destruction level of collapsed mud-brick over a deposit certainly linked with the Palestinian Early Bronze Age, and beneath a levelling over of the site carried out for the purpose of constructing a temple that was in use during the time of the XIIth Dynasty, are burials belonging to an intrusive people. There is no evidence that to these people any structures or defences are to be ascribed, and thus again they would seem in habit to be not far removed from a nomadic way of life. Their burials are found on the original tell (unlikely if there was any intensive urban occupa-

[1] *Ugaritica II*, pp. 64–66.
[2] *Stratigraphie comparée*, pls. v (= *Ugaritica II*, fig. 20 and pl. xii) and viii.

tion at the time) and they also spread over the area surrounding the foot of the tell. The positive links between these burials and E.B.–M.B. Palestine are the pottery vessels found with one burial, and the swollen-headed pins and fenestrated axeheads

RAS SHAMRA.
2ᵉ Niveau
Ugarit Moyen 1
2100-1900

15cm.

. Dessins de G Chenet .

FIG. 22. Selected objects from E.B.–M.B. (*porteurs de torques*) burials at Ras Shamra.

which are taken as type fossils of the period,[1] of which the pins are found at Megiddo and the fenestrated axeheads at Megiddo and Jericho (see above, pp. 30–31).

Schaeffer rightly stresses the point that the *porteurs de torques* were skilled metal-workers. Some of their products, especially the socketed spearheads, give evidence of an advanced technique. Though the actual number of examples found at Ras Shamra cannot be deduced from the published evidence,

[1] Cf. e.g. *Ugaritica II*, p. 55.

the correlations that Schaeffer has made with other Syrian
sites shows that metal-working was an important aspect of the
activities of the newcomers. The Palestinian evidence shows
that this is not a necessary attribute of all the groups that appear
as immigrants in the settled areas at this time; only some groups,
for instance the people buried in the Dagger type tombs at
Jericho, in the 1500 Cemetery at T. Ajjul and at T. Duweir
certainly included metal-workers, though here again the daggers
made by them do not resemble the daggers at Ras Shamra. It
is not here the place to assess the implications of Schaeffer's
demonstration that metal objects amazingly similar to those
found at Ras Shamra can be found right across Europe as far
as Alsace, but it is probable that among the newcomers were
elements akin to the 'tinkers' or gipsies of the modern Near East
who move within, but are not of, the population of the area.

To the evidence of Ras Shamra can be added that of a number
of other sites further inland. Schaeffer has already called attention to the occurrence at them of metal objects similar to those
at Ras Shamra. From the Palestinian point of view, the most
interesting evidence is that at these inland sites is found pottery
that can be linked with some of the aspects of the E.B.–M.B.
period in Palestine, and also the fact that though both at Qatna
and Tell 'As swollen-headed toggle pins of the Ras Shamra
type are found, with at Qatna a dagger of the Ras Shamra type,
the other metal objects are of different types, and they occur in
tombs as a minor constituent compared with the great masses of
pottery vessels. It would seem to be the same picture of linked
but not identical groups.

The site essentially the most important is Qatna, situated
some 18 kilometres north-east of Homs. Even today, though the
name on the map is that of an insignificant village, it stands up
as one approaches it from all sides by reason of the magnificent
surrounding ramparts (Pls. VII. 1 and VIII. 1). These ramparts
belong to a subsequent stage in the history of the site, to which we
shall return. But within them is an earlier nucleus, which can
be identified in the contoured plan of the site,[1] and which appears
in views (Pl. VIII. 2) as an eminence in the western area of the enclosure largely occupied by the modern village. The north-west
part of this eminence is described in the excavation reports as
the *butte de l'Église*. Beneath the structures on this higher area,
of which the history covers the greater part of the second millennium B.C., was found pottery which is closely linked with

[1] *Syria*, vii, pl. LI.

that of the important Tomb IV, though it may well continue later. Evidence concerning the stratification of this mound is not described in enough detail to provide a basis for interpretation, but it is described as a mass of mud-bricks, within which there

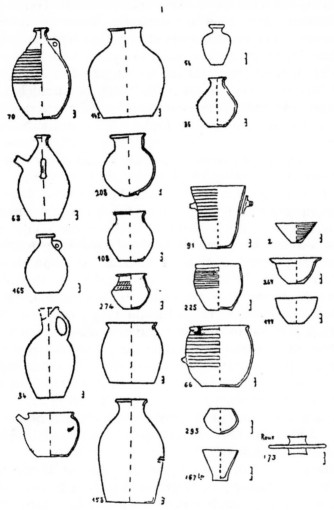

FIG. 23. Pottery from Qatna Tomb IV.

are walls. Presumably therefore it is a typical tell built up of collapsed mud-brick buildings. The relation to the tell of the E.B.–M.B. pottery is quite uncertain.

Qatna Tomb IV contained a large number of pots[1] (Fig. 23) in addition to the metal objects. The family resemblance of many of them to the vessels from the Jericho Outsize tombs is

[1] *Syria*, xi, pls. xxxi–xxxiv.

very apparent; the plump flat-based jars with necks, the wide-mouthed jars likewise with flat bases, and the spouted jars are closely similar. The resemblances to vessels in the Megiddo tombs is perhaps even closer and the beakers are probably related to the beakers in the Megiddo Shaft Tomb 1120B,[1] though there are closer resemblances in vessels from other Syrian sites. The pins include all the four types found in the two kinds of tombs at Megiddo. Only one vessel is surprising on Palestinian evidence, the jug no. 34, which resembles jugs of Early Bronze II in Palestine. The Palestine parallels are thus sufficiently clear and numerous to indicate the general direction from which the immigrants into at least northern Palestine came.

The excavator of Qatna, Count du Mesnil du Buisson, made soundings at a number of other sites in the vicinity or same general area. At Khan Sheikhoun, T. Masin, T. Dnebi, and T. 'As, amongst others, the picture is the same. Between material that is probably Early Bronze Age and material certainly Middle Bronze Age, appears material, mainly in tombs, with clear links with the Palestinian E.B.–M.B. At Khan Sheikhoun, for instance, is one of the closest parallels to the Megiddo beaker.[2] At T. 'As there are in Tomb I vessels (Fig. 24) which most certainly must be related to the very characteristic range of little pots found in the Pottery type tombs at Jericho, while the range of pins exactly parallels those from the two types of tombs at Megiddo. It is interesting that the tomb shaft and chamber are similar to those of some of the Jericho Outsize type tombs, though the shaft is not so deep. Tomb II at T. 'As has a similar tomb form and range of pottery vessels, and a swollen-headed pin of the Ras Shamra type, also found in Megiddo Tomb 1101–2 B Lower.

In the plains of northern Syria, between the Mediterranean and the upper Euphrates, there are thus to be found a number of sites at which the finds suggest links with Ras Shamra on the one hand and Palestine on the other. Excavation has revealed too little of the stratification of the sites for deduction to be made as to the type of occupation; all that can be said is that there is nothing to prove an urban type of culture, and since the groups at Ras Shamra and in Palestine, with which links have been shown, were non-urban, it may be that the occupation

[1] *Megiddo Tombs*, pl. 22. 19.
[2] *Stratigraphie comparée*, fig. 103: Khan Sheikhoun i; *Syria*, xiii, pl. xxxvi. 114.

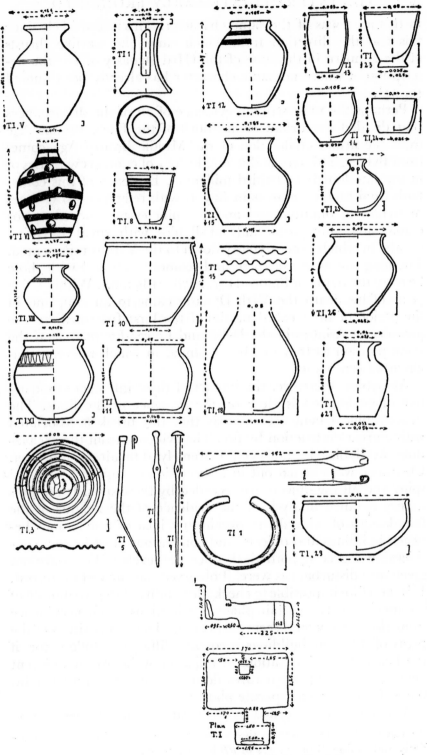

Fig. 24. Pottery and bronzes from T. ʿAs Tomb I.

in this area was of the same character. This is also likely since this was the direction from which came the warlike thrusts of the Amurru in the time of the IIIrd Dynasty of Ur, the description of whose nomadic character has already been quoted (p. 34).

Perhaps the most striking evidence of all of the disturbances that divided the urban civilizations of the Early Bronze Age from the urban civilization of the Middle Bronze Age comes from Byblos. This city had a long history of contacts with Egypt in the late fourth and third millennia. Evidence of this comes both from literary sources in Egypt, with references to voyages to Byblos to obtain wood and the pine-essence necessary for embalming, and from finds at Byblos with royal Egyptian names, in which every dynasty down to the VIth is represented. The long succession of these finds comes to an end with those bearing the name of Phiops II (c. 2278–2185 B.C.). Within a few years of his death the VIth Dynasty came to an end, and in the period of the weak dynasties of the First Intermediate the presence of Asiatics in the Delta and Lower Egypt reflects the same position as that in Mesopotamia, to which reference has already been made.

At Byblos, therefore, the impact of these influences destructive of civilization is clear on the evidence of the finds. The stratigraphical evidence suggests that this break is associated with a great destruction by fire. The evidence from the excavations at Byblos is, however, extremely difficult to interpret. Clearance was carried out in a succession of rigidly horizontal spits, and all the objects are recorded by these spits. It requires a very detailed analysis of the evidence of the heights of the foundations of all walls to obtain any idea of associations between buildings and objects, and conclusions must be to a considerable degree hypothetical, since the levels of floors are not given and disturbances were, if observed, not placed on record. It is therefore impossible to check the validity of the attribution of groups or objects to certain phases, attributions which on evidence from elsewhere would seem surprising.[1] The composition of the plans of different buildings is equally difficult to follow, for, if the bases of the foundations of adjacent walls are at different depths, or the superstructures destroyed to a different height, the walls appear on separate plans.

A major event recorded by the stratification is a destruction

---

[1] e.g. some of the vessels in the pottery groups assigned to phases of the Early and Middle Bronze Ages in *RB* lix, pls. III–VI.

by fire which left a deposit of ash up to 0·50 m. thick over at least the area of the main temple; the extent of this burnt layer is not made clear. Beneath this were the objects that can be dated on epigraphic or other grounds to the time of the Old Kingdom of Egypt; objects with the name of Phiops II were also included in the burnt material. Also beneath it were the comparatively elaborate buildings ascribed by M. Dunand to his *Installation VI*, the beginning of which he correlates chronologically with the time of Khasekhemwy of the IInd Egyptian Dynasty (*c.* 2712–2686 B.C.).[1] This would suggest that the full development of the Early Bronze Age at Byblos coincides with its full development in E.B. III, in Palestine. With this the pottery ascribed to the period agrees, and the very close resemblances show that the Syrian coastal areas and Palestine formed part of the same cultural province at this time;[2] the inadequate stratigraphical record makes it impossible to check those points in the pottery ascriptions in which there is disagreement.

In the area of this temple there was, above the burnt layer, a deposit of imported sand, clearly a levelling up for the overlying pavement of a rebuilt temple that existed early enough to receive offerings in the time of the XIIth Egyptian Dynasty, and continued in use down to Roman times;[3] the stratigraphic record does not provide sufficient evidence to disentangle the features of the building during this very long period.

Byblos therefore suffered a destruction at about the end of the reign of Phiops II, thus at the same period as that in which the incursions of Asiatics into Egypt broke up settled government and created the conditions that existed in the First Intermediate. It is legitimate to assume that the cause was the same.

This break M. Dunand ascribes without hesitation[4] to the advent of the Amorites. To these new-comers he ascribes the very much simpler structures, *logis monocellulaires*, that succeeded those of his *Installation VI*. He suggests that these simple structures begin to appear a little before the great destruction by fire.[5] It might be permitted to query whether this claimed overlap may not be due to the lack of exact stratigraphical evidence; the published details do not allow one to decide.

There is also not adequate evidence to allow an assessment

---

[1] *RB* lix.  [2] *Ibid.*, pls. III–V.

[3] A schematic section reconstructing the succession of deposits has been given by Schaeffer in *Stratigraphie comparée*, pl. XVIII.

[4] *RB* lix.  [5] *Ibid.*, p. 86.

to be made of the stratigraphic position of a very remarkable collection of deposits grouped in areas that were clearly sacred over a very long period; many of the objects in these deposits are certainly to be related to Schaeffer's *porteurs de torques* and to the period here called Intermediate Early Bronze–Middle Bronze—a term that says much the same thing as Schaeffer's *Zone de contact des Niveaux II et III.*[1]

These deposits are concentrated in three areas, that of the temple M. Dunand calls the Temple of the Baalat (otherwise called *Bâtiment II* or the Syrian Temple), the Temple of the Obelisks (otherwise called the Temple of Reshif), and the temple of the area called the *Champs des Offrandes.* In each case there is believed to have been a temple on the site during the Early Bronze Age, rebuilt after a destruction and in use from the time of the XIIth Egyptian Dynasty down to the Roman period. Unfortunately, the evidence provided does not enable one to assign the architectural remains to exact periods, nor in many cases to say quite certainly to which successive structures the deposits belong. It can reasonably be assumed from their character, groups of metal objects carefully placed in pots, and concentration in particular areas, that they are offerings or ceremonial deposits buried within sacred areas, but without an exact stratigraphical record it cannot be said whether any one deposit was contemporary with the construction of any building or was dug into the floor during the life of the building, or even was already in the soil into which the walls were dug and therefore belonged to an earlier building. It can certainly not be proved that all the deposits in any one area are contemporary, and need not be assumed. There do in fact seem to be some differences in character, which may be very important in the history of the culture in Byblos.

The first deposits to be found were in the Temple of the Baalat, where to the well-known jar of M. Montet[2] were added three others in M. Dunand's subsequent excavations.[3] The container of one of the latter, jar 2132,[4] was of a form which in Palestine would be Early Bronze Age. The contents[5] were almost entirely objects of types selected by Schaeffer as characteristic of the equipment of his *porteurs de torques*, a fenestrated axehead, watch-spring spirals, swollen-headed toggle pins,

[1] *Stratigraphie comparée*, pl. XVIII.
[2] *Byblos et l'Égypte*, pls. LX–LXXI.
[3] *Byblos I*, pp. 81–84, 137–41.
[4] *Byblos I*, pl. LXV.          [5] *Ibid.*, pls. LXV–LXXI.

torcs with curled ends, heavy bracelets, daggers with triangular hilts (Pls. IX and X). In addition, there were long pointed daggers near those of E.B.–M.B. Jericho and T. Ajjul, flat celts (Pl. IX), and an interesting series of bronze and silver vessels, to which we shall return. It can hardly be doubted that this deposit is contemporary with the E.B.–M.B. stage at Ras Shamra already discussed.

The Montet jar (Pl. XI. 2) contained many similar objects, scores of bracelets and torcs (Pl. XII), swollen-headed toggle pins, biconical beads (Pl. XIII), and again bronze bowls (Pl. XIV). But in addition there were a large number of scarabs, in which this deposit was unique among the thirty-five or so discovered. These have been compared by Albright[1] to the sealings found by Reisner at Uronarti and dated to the first half of the XIIIth Dynasty; if this dating is to be accepted, it is strange that the Byblos range is so very limited, and the patterns so very simple, compared with the contemporary scarabs from Palestine, for instance in the Jericho sequence.[2] As will be seen, there is strong reason for giving a terminal date for the Byblos deposits as a whole of not later than early in the time of the XIIth Dynasty. This reasoning, based on the general archaeological evidence, is now supported by the views of Miss O. Tufnell (to be published shortly), based on stylistic grounds, that the scarabs belong to the period of the First Intermediate in Egypt.

The other two of Dunand's deposits came not from the temple itself but from an adjacent masonry massif in the form of a truncated pyramid in which there were two niches to hold the jars. One jar, 2000, was barrel-shaped and in the Early Bronze Age tradition, the other, 2064, round-based and more allied to Middle Bronze vessels (Pl. XV). Jar 2000 contained a bronze juglet in a form resembling that of Middle Bronze Age pottery juglets, and besides that a mass of little bronze figurines, 77 in all (Pls. XVI. 1 and 2). Five were of animals, but the rest were human, two women but all the others men, mostly naked with peaked caps, some completely naked, and some with kilts. Most were in the round, but a few were silhouettes only. Jar 2064 contained only figurines of little men, of similar types.

The 22 deposits in the *Champs des Offrandes* were mostly contained in elongated barrel-shaped jars (Pls. XVII, XIX. 2). M. Dunand suggests with considerable probability that these were specially made for the purpose; their general appearance

---

[1] *AASOR* xiii, p. 74.
[2] D. Kirkbride in *Jericho II*, Appendix F.

suggests an Early Bronze Age tradition. Many of the deposits contained bronze figurines (Pls. XVIII. 1, 2, XIX. 1), of the types already described. Others had weapons as well, fenestrated axes (and some of the little men carry these axes), varieties of short daggers, socketed spearheads (Pls. XVIII. 2, XIX. 1, 2), and a few javelins (Pl. XIX. 2)[1] with curled tips to the tang, allied to those found in E.B.–M.B. tombs at Jericho,[2] T. Duweir,[3] and T. Ajjul.[4] Some had weapons, of this range, alone. A few had swollen-headed toggle pins and there were also a few torcs with curled ends (Pl. XX. 1).

The deposits in the Obelisk Temple are related to the last group by the presence of many figurines of the same type. There were also torcs with curled ends, fenestrated axes, and short daggers with triangular hilts. But in these there is an important difference, for most of them are in gold or silver[5] (Pl. XX. 2). This is of particular significance in the case of the weapons, for clearly they are ceremonial and non-functional. Another way in which these groups differ from those in the two other areas is the presence in some of them of figurines of obvious Egyptian inspiration if not manufacture,[6] of types probably belonging to the XIIth or XIIIth Dynasty. In one group there are a number of vessels of glazed paste, some of which are certainly of the form of Middle Bronze Age pottery vessels, and vessels in other groups, in pottery or metal, also are Middle Bronze in form.

It may thus be possible to suggest a sequence, though this must be hypothetical for lack of stratigraphic evidence. The group that is most firmly related to Schaeffer's *porteurs de torques* is that in jar 2132 in the Temple of the Baalat. It contains a rich collection of Schaeffer's characteristic objects and nothing that is discordant. It can therefore be called E.B.–M.B. A few of the deposits in the *Champs des Offrandes* have similar weapons, but in less profusion. The next group would be those with similar weapons, and some other objects, but with the addition of the bronze figurines. In the third group, that in the Obelisk Temple, the figurines continue, but there are enough objects suggesting the renewed contacts with Egypt that began with the XIIth Dynasty and other objects suggesting a Middle Bronze Age date. There are still weapons of E.B.–M.B. form, notably the fenestrated axes, but their

---

[1] *Byblos II*, pl. LXV, LXVIII, &c.    [2] *Jericho II*, fig. 41.
[3] *Lachish IV*, pl. 21.    [4] *Ancient Gaza I*, pl. XIX. 48, 49.
[5] *Byblos II*, pls. CXX, CXXXIII, CXXXIV, CXXXVI, &c.
[6] *Byblos II*, pls. XCIV–CVIII.

precious metal and beautiful decoration show them to be ceremonial and for this reason preserving an archaic form.

It thus seems that these deposits bridge the period from the
end of the Early Bronze Age to the beginning of the Middle
Bronze Age and equally from the end of Old Kingdom influence
in Byblos to the beginning of Middle Kingdom influence.
Almost the only piece of firm stratigraphical evidence is that
the deposits in the Temple of the Baalat overlie the burnt layer
beneath which and in which are objects with the name of
Phiops II (c. 2278–2185 B.C.). The bearers of the new culture, with
the new type of objects, thus arrived at Byblos at the end of the
twenty-third or beginning of the twenty-second century B.C. At
Byblos, as elsewhere in Syria, they introduced a new way of
life, with house-plans of a much simpler type. But it seems probable that the strong urban tradition of Byblos must have
civilized them in a way for which there is no evidence elsewhere
(except in Palestine at Megiddo). It would seem that their
houses were widespread over the site of the earlier town, though
scattered and irregularly orientated,[1] and the sequence of deposits in the sacred areas suggests that they rebuilt the temples,
or even, since at least in some cases the evidence for underlying
Early Bronze Age temples is not very clear, built them as new
foundations. The practice of making deposits including the
characteristic little men continued down to the time when
Egyptian influence begins to reappear. But the date of the latest
of them cannot be put too far into the period of renewed Egyptian influence. Very useful dating evidence is provided by the
contents of the Royal Tombs,[2] for Tomb I, that of Abichemou,
is dated by inscriptions to the reign of Ammenemes III (1842–
1797 B.C.), and Tomb II, that of Ip Chemou Abi, to the reign
of Ammenemes IV (1798–1790 B.C.), the last king but one of the
XIIth Dynasty. The pottery in these tombs (Pls. XXI. 1, 2) is
fully developed Middle Bronze, quite unlike anything found
even with the deposits that would appear to be the latest in the
material just discussed. This material can date therefore at latest
to the beginning of the XIIth Dynasty, early in the twentieth
century B.C.

The pottery of these Royal Tombs at Byblos provides an important link with the succeeding Middle Bronze Age. As will
be seen, in this period there is a culture which, on the evidence
of the pottery, is entirely new at many of the sites at which it

---

[1] *RB* lix, p. 85.
[2] *Byblos et l'Égypte*, pp. 143–204, pls. LXXXVIII–CXIX.

appears. At Ras Shamra as at every site in Palestine new and flourishing towns appear, and the pottery owes nothing to that of earlier periods. The evidence of the pottery is the most striking, but there are equally marked differences in other objects. This pottery is found the length of the Syro-Palestinian coast, but not in inland Syria. It is thus the pottery of the Canaanite area, for Kinahna is the name given to the area in Akkadian texts from the trade in purple dye for which it was famed. In the evolution of this new culture, which can thus be called Canaanite, Byblos may have played a major part, a suggestion to which we shall return in the next chapter.

# III

## THE CANAANITES IN PALESTINE AND SYRIA

ONCE again, it is convenient to start consideration of the new period in Palestine, for here the evidence is much more fully available, and possibly more clear-cut, for this period again is separated by a sharp break from the preceding one.

The clearest evidence that the urban civilization of the Middle Bronze Age does not evolve from the Intermediate Early Bronze–Middle Bronze period comes from the pottery. In place of the drab-coloured vessels of the E.B.–M.B. pottery, the vast majority of jars of a not very great variety of forms, with the characteristic technique of a hand-made body and a wheel-made rim, there appear vessels of a wide range of shapes, made on a fast wheel, and very often with a highly burnished red slip (Fig. 25). The occurrences of this type of pottery are not widespread; the main groups come from T. Beit Mirsim, strata G–F,[1] the T. Ajjul Courtyard Cemetery,[2] and Ras el 'Ain.[3] At Megiddo, vessels of similar forms appear, though there are some different varieties, and there is a greater use of painted bands in place of the burnished red slip. The reasons for these differences are discussed below. At Jericho, in the restricted area in which Middle Bronze Age structures have survived denudation, finds of this period occur only in a tomb which, unlike the extra-mural ones belonging to Middle Bronze II, was on the tell and was built of mud-bricks. The impression given by these finds, so very restricted in comparison with those of the succeeding period, is of a gradual infiltration in small numbers rather than of a large-scale invasion.

The relation of this pottery to that found in coastal Syria is clear. Reference has already been made to the Royal Tombs at Byblos,[4] dated by inscriptions belonging to rulers of Byblos, contemporary respectively with Ammenemes III (1842–1797 B.C.) and Ammenemes IV (1798–1790 B.C.) of the XIIth Egyptian Dynasty. Jars, bowls, and juglets in these tombs are closely similar to those of Middle Bronze I in Palestine.[5] Another group

---

[1] *AASOR* xii, pl. 41. 1–9 and xiii, pls. 4 and 5.
[2] *Ancient Gaza II.*    [3] *QDAP* v and vi.
[4] *Byblos et l'Égypte*, pp. 143–204, pls. LXXVIII–CXIX.
[5] Since I advocate the use of the term Intermediate Early Bronze–Middle

of similar pottery has been found at Kafr Djarra, near Sidon,[1] of similar form and shape.

It is partly on the basis of the forms of this pottery, especially

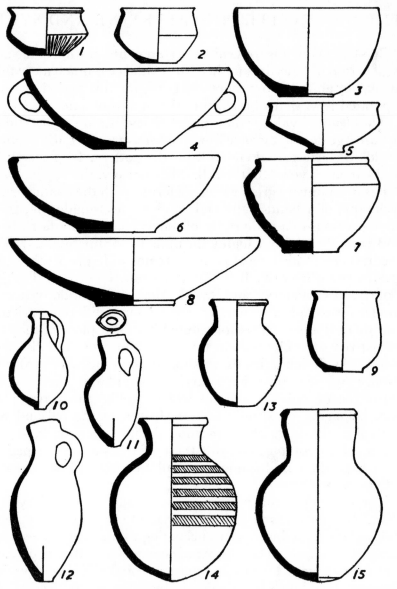

Fig. 25. Pottery of Middle Bronze I from Ras el 'Ain (2–4, 6–10, 13–15) and T. Ajjul (1, 5, 11–12). $\frac{1}{5}$

Bronze for the period that follows the end of the Early Bronze Age, the succeeding period becomes Middle Bronze I, though Albright and his school prefer to call the E.B.–M.B. period M.B. I, and this period M.B. IIa.

[1] *Stratigraphie comparée*, fig. 75.

the bowls, that the suggestion is here put forward that it was at Byblos that this culture emerged. Professor Albright long ago pointed out that the sharply angular form of the bowls demands a not far-distant metal prototype,[1] and he subsequently suggested[2] that such a prototype was to be found in a bowl in the deposit found by M. Montet in the Temple of the Baalat (or *Bâtiment II*);[3] another similar bowl occurs in jar 2132 near by[4] (see above, p. 49). This is very plausible, though for reasons given above (p. 51) it is unlikely that the bowl is as late as Albright suggests.

Another reason for assigning this ancestral position to Byblos is that out of the plain, short, triangular-shaped dagger found in the E.B.–M.B. period at Ras Shamra[5] (cf. Fig. 22. 3–4) and Byblos (cf. Pl. IX),[6] so different from the long thin daggers of the Palestinian E.B.–M.B. period, seems to be evolved the short triangular dagger with the veined marking of the midrib[7] to which the typical dagger of the Palestinian M.B. I stage is clearly related[8] (Pl. II. 1. 9), and from which the M.B. II daggers develop (Fig. 26).

It is, however, possible that in the initial stages of the Middle Bronze Age in Palestine another strain is to be recognized. The Middle Bronze I pottery at Megiddo[9] (Fig. 27) has points of contact with that from the other sites of the period, notably the hemispherical flat-based bowls[10] and the sharply carinated bowls,[11] and in the plump form of the juglets. But these latter usually have a decoration of painted bands[12] instead of a burnished red slip, and another characteristic form is a bowl with a thickened

[1] *AASOR* xii, pp. 14–15.  
[2] *AASOR* xiii, p. 69.  
[3] *Byblos et l'Égypte*, pl. LXXI.  
[4] *Byblos I*, pl. LXVI.  
[5] *Ugaritica II*, fig. 18, *Ugarit-Moyen*, i.  
[6] e.g. *Byblos I*, pl. LXX from jar 2132; *Byblos II*, pls. LXII and LXVIII from the *Champs des Offrandes*.  
[7] e.g. *Byblos II*, 10828–31.  
[8] e.g. *Ancient Gaza II*, pl. XIV; *Megiddo II*, pl. 178.  
[9] The characteristics of this are not immediately apparent in the publication of *Megiddo II*, since most of it comes from graves, the contents of which, owing to the inadequate stratigraphical observations, were assigned to the level to which the base of the grave penetrated instead of that from which the grave was dug. The consistency of the material is, however, well shown in the tomb groups published in *Megiddo Tombs*, e.g. Tombs 911 A 1, 912 B, 912 D. When the burials on the tell are analysed into groups, they exhibit the same consistent range of pottery, &c.  
[10] e.g. *Megiddo Tombs*, pl. 28. 24–31; pl. 31. 15.  
[11] e.g. *ibid.*, pl. 28. 36–38.  
[12] e.g. *ibid.*, 29. 1–4; pl. 35. 6–8.

rim.[1] These forms are more closely related to vessels found in inland Syria, of which a typical group is seen in Qatna Tomb I[2] (Fig. 28). Here also are found jugs with upward-pointing lips and juglets with a disk below the rim, not found elsewhere in Palestine; the characteristic jar form is handleless, which is also

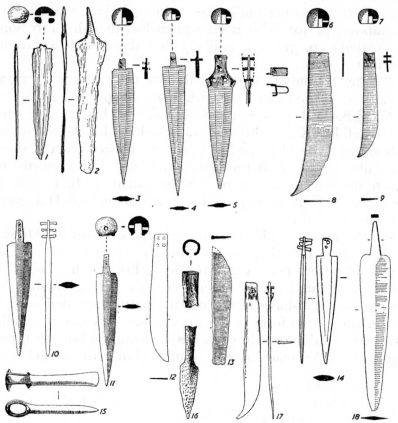

FIG. 26. Weapons and tools of Middle Bronze II, from Jericho. c. $\frac{1}{7}$

found at Megiddo, and though there are examples at Ras el 'Ain, it is rare in Palestine. Juglets very similar to those at Megiddo are also found at Ras Shamra (Fig. 29).[3]

It is, however, significant that in Palestine, and probably also at Ras Shamra, it is from the types of pottery allied to those of Byblos that those of the succeeding period evolve. Even at Megiddo, the elaborate forms of M.B. I soon die out, and for the later periods here and for all other sites there is a continuous

[1] e.g. fig. 27. 5–6 (*Megiddo Tombs*, pl. 28. 1–21).
[2] *Syria*, xi, pls. XXXI–XXXIV; the date suggested is certainly too late.
[3] e.g. *Ugaritica II*, fig. 99. 18–22; fig. 100. 6–9, 12–16.

and close succession of forms and technique from the type of
pottery found in the groups cited from T. Beit Mirsim, T. Ajjul,

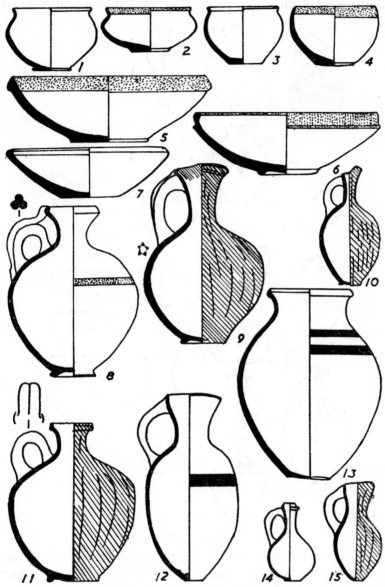

FIG. 27. Middle Bronze I Pottery from Megiddo. ⅕

and Ras el 'Ain. The succession is well shown at Jericho, where
it has been possible to establish a sequence of pottery assem-
blages (Figs. 30–32) covering the period from c. 1800 B.C. to the
early sixteenth century.[1]

[1] The only absolute dating comes from the relatively few scarabs which

In Syria, this is the pottery of the coastal area. On the rather limited evidence from the inland sites such as Qatna, the line of development diverges from that of Palestine. But at Ras

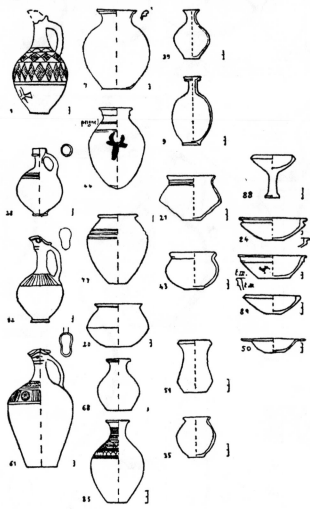

FIG. 28. Pottery from Qatna Tomb I.

Shamra, though there were the initial contacts with the inland area already mentioned, the pottery forms are very closely similar to those in Palestine[1] (Fig. 33).

Thus it would seem that this culture, of which the pottery is the evidence, developed in coastal Syria, in the region centred on Byblos. In Palestine and at Ras Shamra it was superimposed

can be given a definite Egyptian date. See D. Kirkbride in *Jericho II*, pp. 592–3.

[1] e.g. *Ugaritica II*, fig. 105, *Tombe, Tr. est cône, pointe topographique* 19.

on the pre-existing culture without any development therefrom. It thus developed in a most important area of the land known to the Akkadians as Kinahna, derived from the purple dye for

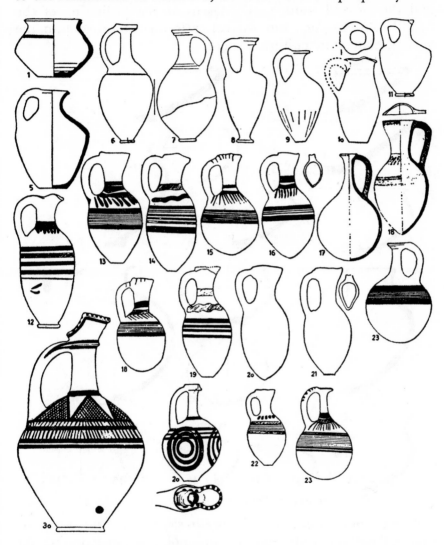

FIG. 29. Selected Middle Bronze I pottery from Ras Shamra.

which it was famed, to the Greeks as Phoenicia, a name which to them meant the same though formed by a false assimilation of their root φοινικ with Egyptian *Fnh.w* meaning woodworkers, since it was for this that the area was famous to the Egyptians; the culture can therefore be called Canaanite.

It is also reasonable to suggest that the pottery that developed at Qatna became characteristic of the Amorites of the second

millennium B.C., owing something to shared influences in the
initial stages, but thereafter diverging. Megiddo may have had
an incursion from the inland area via the Plain of Esdraelon
and the age-old route to Damascus at the beginning of the
Middle Bronze Age, but thereafter it was absorbed into the
general Canaanite cultural sphere.

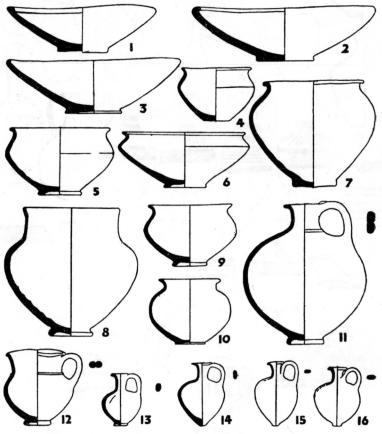

Fig. 30. Pottery of Middle Bronze II phase i at Jericho. ⅕

There is not yet enough evidence to say how the superimposi-
tion of the new culture upon the old took place in Palestine. As
already stated,[1] evidence of M.B. I is found only on a few sites.
Unless this is an accident of excavation, it suggests a small-
scale infiltration. The country-wide spread of which the distribution of M.B. II pottery is evidence may have taken place
by expansion from a few original centres, or perhaps more likely
by the adoption by the inhabitants of the more advanced culture
they saw in their midst. The land of Canaan of the Books of

[1] P. 53.

Exodus and Joshua was thus established. What it is not possible to say is why the inhabitants of some towns still regarded them-

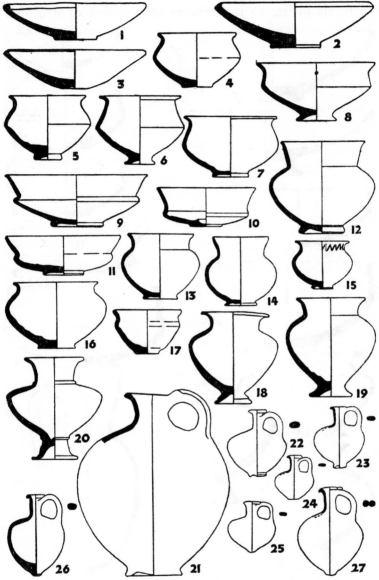

FIG. 31. Pottery of Middle Bronze II phase iii at Jericho. $\frac{1}{5}$

selves as Amorite some five hundred years later. It may be something to do with how they acquired the Canaanite culture, whether by absorption or by being captured.

The great advance in civilization is shown by all sites excavated. Once more, an urban civilization with closely built-up

towns surrounded by imposing defences is found. T. Beit Mirsim
was certainly a town in M.B. I.[1] This was probably also the
case at Megiddo, though the confusion of plans between different levels owing to inadequate observation of stratification

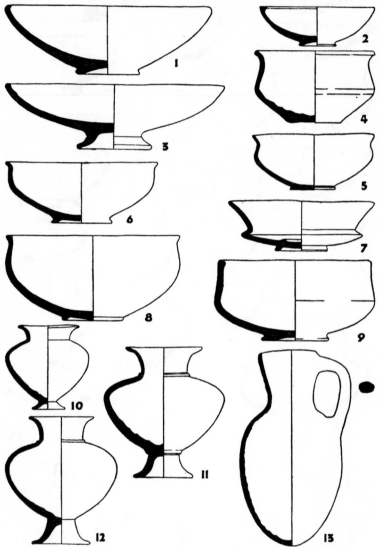

FIG. 32. Pottery of Middle Bronze II phase v at Jericho. $\frac{1}{5}$

makes the ascription of buildings to the period impossible.
T. Ajjul, T. Fara, T. Duweir, T. el Far'ah (near Nablus), Jericho,
and many other sites were fully developed towns at least by
M.B. II. In Syria, too, the process was the same, at least on the

[1] AASOR xvii, pp. 17–25, Stratum G–F

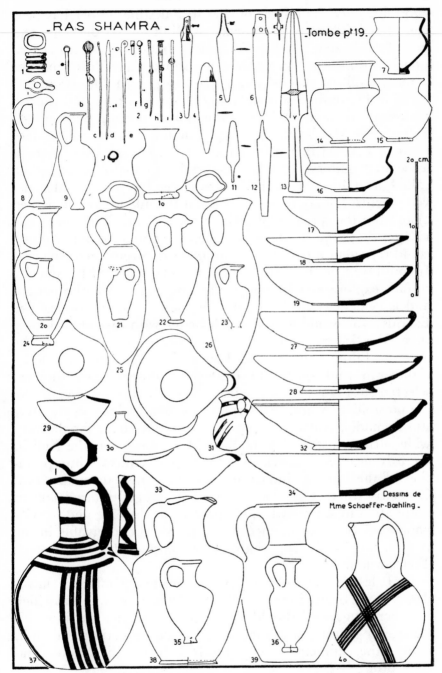

FIG. 33. Pottery from Ras Shamra *Tombe est cône, pointe topographique 19.*

evidence of Ras Shamra; unfortunately very little is known of the plans of other sites, though if the evidence of Byblos could be disentangled, it would certainly show the same thing.

So far, only the history of sites in Palestine proper has been considered. There is no evidence at all of similar developments east of the Jordan. For long it was said that there was no occupation in Transjordan in the Middle Bronze Age. This would be a most unlikely state of affairs. In 1953, a Middle Bronze II tomb from Amman was published,[1] but it is true that this remains an isolated and exceptional example of finds of the Palestinian Middle Bronze Age. On the other hand, surface finds of E.B.–M.B. material there are common. Also there is associated material of types of vessels not found in Palestine, called by Glueck E.B. IV,[2] which could represent later developments. It may be suggested that the inland area remained aloof from the spread of the Canaanite culture. The towns and villages that grew up there, in which the pottery is of this type,[3] could represent a parallel development that remained Amorite. It could well be that much of the pottery collected in Glueck's surface explorations belongs to this prolonged Amorite period, and is evidence of the Amorite kingdoms of the period of the Exodus; this would accord much better with the Biblical story than Glueck's conclusion that there was no occupation in the area of Edom, Moab, and Gilead between the twentieth-eighteenth and thirteenth centuries.[4] Proper excavation of selected sites is urgently needed to see whether this hypothesis is a possibility. A similar interpretation of a prolonged, and here still nomadic, Amorite occupation would account for the very wide surface distribution of E.B.–M.B. pottery in the Negeb; there is certainly no evidence to support Glueck's interpretation of the finds as indicating a great vanished civilization.[5] Otherwise there must have been a prolonged intermission in occupation at a time when Cisjordan was thriving and heavily populated. Such an absence of occupation is conceivable in the Negeb, but highly improbable in the fertile plains of western Transjordan.

In Palestine west of the Jordan, the main influence introduced at the beginning of the Middle Bronze Age was that which it is here suggested should be called Canaanite. But into this Canaanite culture, or in some cases perhaps superimposed on it, many other influences were absorbed during the Middle and Late Bronze Age.

[1] *APEF* vi.    [2] e.g. *AASOR* xviii–xix, p. 251.
[3] e.g. in the excavations of P. J. Parr at Iskander.
[4] *AASOR* xv, p. 138; *AASOR* xviii–xix, p. 268.
[5] *Rivers in the Desert*, p. 11, &c.

The Middle Bronze Age, particularly the eighteenth–seventeenth centuries, was a period of movements of peoples. It is not comparable with the explosive spread of the Amorites in the last centuries of the second millennium, for the basic culture, as evidenced by the towns and material equipment, of coastal Syria and Palestine remains the same. But it is the period during which the Ḫabiru begin to appear and of the great Ḫurrian spread, while by c. 1730 B.C. the infiltration of the Asiatics into the Egyptian delta had grown to such proportions that the domination of the so-called Hyksos, the hated 'rulers of foreign lands', brought the Middle Kingdom to an end and ushered in the Second Intermediate.

The extent of the Ḫurrian spread is such that by the time of the Amarna letters belonging to the first third of the fourteenth century B.C., the names of many of the rulers of towns in Syria and Palestine were Ḫurrian. Ḫurrian names are also found in Egypt in the Second Intermediate. But the greater number of names and words are Semitic, and clearly the dominating element among the Hyksos was Semitic. To this the Ḫabiru may have contributed, for the most reasonable interpretation of references to them and to the probably allied 'Apiru of Egypt is that they were bands of stateless people, warrior-bands, sometimes mercenaries, sometimes enslaved as prisoners of war, recruited from numerous sources, including the great reservoir of semi-nomads on the fringes of the Arabian desert.

That Palestine must have been concerned in movements of Asiatic groups into Egypt is demanded by geography. It has become customary to refer to the material culture of Palestine in Middle Bronze II as Hyksos. But it has been shown that there is absolutely no break in such diagnostic equipment as pottery from Middle Bronze I. The basic culture remains the same, and it is quite misleading to associate one stage of it with the warlike Hyksos of mixed origin.

It is in fact in connexion with warfare that the arrival of a new influence is most clearly seen in both Palestine and Syria. During the course of the Middle Bronze Age a complely new system of fortifications is introduced, that of a bank surmounted by a wall instead of a free-standing wall.

The evidence from Jericho on this subject is particularly clear. The remains of the houses of the Middle Bronze Age only survived in a small area, and were only investigated in their lower levels in a still more restricted area. But here it was clear that a number of building stages were associated with a succession of walls, free-standing walls of mud-brick in the tradition of those in the Early Bronze Age.[1] To this succeeded something much more imposing. From a stone revetment at the base (Pl. XXII. 1), a bank elaborately faced with plaster (Pl. XXII. 2), keyed-in to the bank-fill (Pl. XXIII. 1), sloped up at an angle of 35° to a wall at the summit, of which only the foundations survived. There were three stages to the bank and to the revetment at the foot; in the final stages, all the early deposits outside the line of the revetment were stripped to bedrock and the total height from the foot of the revetment to the foundations on the

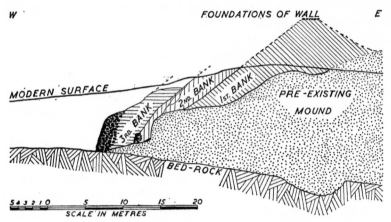

FIG. 34. Reconstructed section of Middle Bronze II rampart at Jericho.

summit was, on the combined evidence of two areas, *c.* 46 ft., and the spread between these points 66 ft. In the areas investigated by the 1952–8 expedition, only evidence concerning the outer slope of these defences was obtained. Here the bank was backed against, and superimposed on, the mound that had been built up during the earlier periods of occupation. But it could be observed elsewhere that the bank was also upstanding on the inner, town side. A reconstructed section of the defences as they must have existed on the north, west, and south sides of the town is shown on Fig. 34. On the fourth side, however, the massive revetment that formed the foot of the bank was traced by the Austro-German expedition swinging out to the east.[2] It thus swings out into the plain for a distance of some 150 ft. in front of the defences of the earlier period, and it thus would have been a bank upstanding to its full height as it was in other sites, certainly Qatna and T. el Yahudiyeh, to be described below.

----

[1] To be published in *Jericho III.*        [2] *Jericho 1907–1909.*

This form of bank defence, erroneously described as a glacis, is known at a number of other sites in Palestine. At T. Duweir the parallel of the plastered bank is very close (Pl. XXIII. 2). At Jericho there was certainly no exterior ditch. At T. Duweir there was what is known as the Fosse, in which there was the famous Late Bronze Age Fosse Temple, but it hardly merits the name, for it is little more than a flattening of the rock to increase the slope of the bank, with an outer edge of negligible proportions.

At T. Ajjul (Pl. XXIV. 1)[1] and T. Fara (Pl. XXIV. 2),[2] however, there would appear to have been a ditch at the foot of the bank. T. Jeriseh is another site with a similar form of defences,[3] and possibly the traces of plastered slopes at T. Beit Mirsim[4] and those at Megiddo[5] ascribed to Strata XIII and XI in Area AA are to be similarly interpreted.

The most important site, and the one which best shows the association of this phase in Palestine with that elsewhere, is Hazor. The site, with its maximum expansion of *c.* 182 acres overall, is one of the largest in Palestine. In Joshua xi. 10, it is referred to as the 'head of all those cities', showing that in the early stages of the Israelite penetration it was a site of very great importance. The excavations of Professor Yadin and his colleagues[6] shows that to an original tell there was added on the north in Middle Bronze II a great area enclosed by a rampart and, where necessary, a ditch (Pl. XXV). The excavations show both that this was not simply an enclosure, as was suggested by Professor Garstang, who was the first to identify this site as Hazor, but was a fully built-up town, and also that this only took place in Middle Bronze II. The town on this scale continued down into the thirteenth century B.C., but thereafter the Iron Age town, which was preceded by a period of abandonment, shrank back to the area of the original tell. This period of introduction of a new type of defence was thus associated with a considerable increase in town size.

This phenomenon of defences incorporating a massive earth rampart and a greatly increased size of town can certainly be paralleled in at least two sites in Syria. The most impressive is Qatna. Standing up to be seen from miles away (Pls. VII. 1, VIII. 1) are the ramparts of a great rectangular enclosure, a

---

[1] *Ancient Gaza I*, p. 2, pl. XII, top left.
[2] *Beth-pelet I*, pp. 15–17, pl. XIII; *Beth-pelet II*, pl. XLVI.
[3] *QDAP* x.  [4] *AASOR* xvii, pp. 27–29.
[5] *Megiddo II*, pp. 6 and 15.  [6] See *Hazor I–III*.

kilometre long in each direction, with an area of *c.* 247 acres, resembling, to western eyes, nothing so much as a Roman camp, but
with the ramparts surviving on a vastly larger scale (Pl. VII. 2).
One can today see a plaster facing of the ramparts, similar to
that of Jericho and T. Duweir. In the south-west corner of this
great enclosure is a mound, now largely occupied by the modern
village (Pl. VIII. 2). The excavations of Count du Mesnil du Buisson[1] showed that there was here occupation at least as early as the
third millennium, and lasting down into the Late Bronze Age,
when the town was destroyed by Shubbiluliuma in *c.* 1360.
Reference has already been made to the tombs of the E.B.–M.B.
period dug into this mound. There has not yet been sufficient
excavation on the site to show whether, when the great ramparts left the site of the original settlement as an insignificant
pimple in one corner, the whole area was built up, as at Hazor,
but this seems at least possible.

The story at Ras Shamra seems to be similar. The great
trapezoidal enclosure, in area *c.* 47 acres, appears to have in its
north-west corner an original tell, as suggested above (p. 38).
Outside the area to this tell there are graves of the E.B.–M.B.,
or *porteurs de torques*, period, but the first true occupation is of
a period well advanced in the Middle Bronze Age. Even the
prolonged excavations of M. Schaeffer have only investigated
a small part of this whole area. But wherever the excavations
have revealed the sequence, they have shown, on the original
tell and on the area at its foot, that there was a well-laid-out
town with houses on a considerable scale (Fig. 35). The plan of
these houses, with their incorporated underlying tomb-chambers,
is most interesting, but it is not the place to discuss it here.

Other sites in Syria were probably surrounded by similar
ramparts. This can certainly be suggested in the case of Khan
Sheikhoun, between Hama and Aleppo (Pl. XXVI. 1). This was
investigated by soundings only,[2] but the very steep edge of the
mound and the recorded observation in the soundings on its
edge of a fill up to 9 m. thick of pebbles and rammed clay
suggest very strongly that the profile of the mound was created
by an artificial bank similar to that at Jericho. The air photo-
graph even suggests that this rampart is still upstanding on the
inner side.

The sites with these ramparts to which reference has so far
been made are all in Palestine and Syria. They are shown on the
distribution map Fig. 36. It should, however, be noted that at

[1] *Syria,* vii–ix.          [2] *Syria,* xiii.

Qatna, Khan Sheikhoun, and other sites in inland Syria where it is very probable that there are similar ramparts, but which

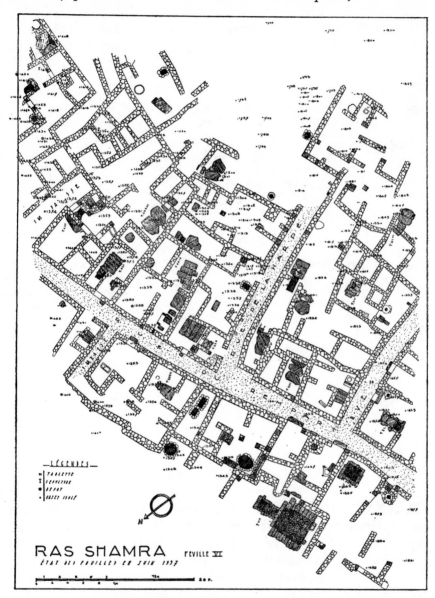

FIG. 35. Plan of houses in lower town at Ras Shamra.

have not yet been sufficiently excavated, the pottery and other finds show that the culture in the Middle Bronze Age diverged from that of coastal Syria and Palestine; on the present thesis, these sites lay outside the area of the Canaanite culture.

More emphatic evidence that this type of defence extended

beyond the cultural area can be adduced. The clearest is that of
T. el Yahudiyeh in Lower Egypt about 20 miles north of Cairo.
Here there is a great rectangular enclosure, investigated by Sir
Flinders Petrie,[1] with ramparts c. 1500 by 1600 ft. (Fig. 37),
standing up above the surrounding plains to a height of c. 41 ft.

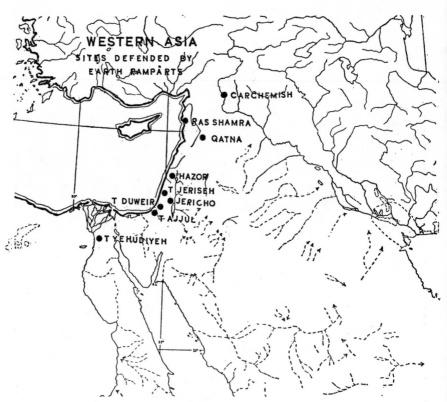

FIG. 36. Distribution map of sites with earth ramparts.

(Pl. XXVI. 2). The 'stucco' revetment of the sand ramparts is
clearly similar to the plaster revetment of Jericho and T. Duweir.
Again, one is forcibly reminded of a Roman camp. Very little
is known of what existed in the interior of the area enclosed by
the ramparts. But finds in graves show that the occupation was
contemporary with the Palestinian Middle Bronze Age, for the
contents made so well known the piriform juglets with pointillé
decoration that they are called 'Tell el Yahudiyeh juglets', and
these are one of the most constant features of the earlier stages
of M.B. II in Palestine. But with these vessels are found, in a

[1] *Hyksos and Israelite Cities.*

great majority, vessels that are purely Egyptian. There were links with Palestine, but the general culture was quite different.

To the north of the Syrian–Palestinian area is Carchemish,[1] There, an 'acropolis' area on the Euphrates had abutting on it an inner town, and abutting on this again is an outer town (Fig. 38). The outer town is Iron Age in origin. The inner town is not very clearly dated. But the construction of its ramparts

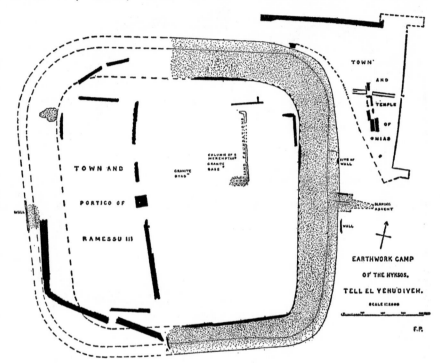

Fig. 37. Plan of T. el Yahudiyeh.

(Pl. XXVI. 3), an upstanding bank built up to a height of 20 m. of layers of brick clay and shingly gravel, with a face at an angle of 30°, revetted with brick clay, is clearly very similar in construction to the ramparts at Jericho, T. Duweir, T. el Yahudiyeh and elsewhere, and other evidence points to a similar date. The 'acropolis' on the river bank, it may be suggested, was, as elsewhere, the original tell to which these defences added a much larger flat area.

The defences of this type, quite new to Palestine and Syria, thus cover an area that is much wider than that of any one cultural group. They provide the evidence of a superimposed feature that, from its military character, may be taken as

[1] *Carchemish II, The Town Defences.*

evidence of a ruling warrior aristocracy. The evidence is not yet sufficient to correlate this with the evidence, from the Amarna letters (see above, p. 65) that there were in Palestine

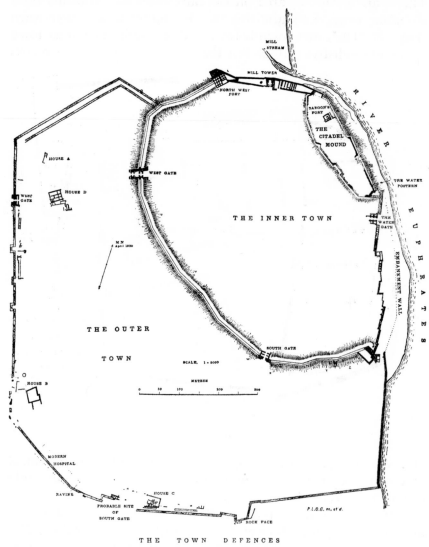

THE   TOWN   DEFENCES

FIG. 38. Plan of Carchemish.

at a later period a number of rulers with Hurrian names. With this phenomenon may go the appearance in the sixteenth century B.C. of a type of bichrome pottery[1] for which Hurrian associations have been suggested.

[1] Studied by W. A. Heurtley. *QDAP* viii, 'A Palestinian Vase-Painter of the Sixteenth Century B.C.' His ascription of this pottery to 'the Ajjul potter'

Perhaps the least compromising name to use for these new features is Hyksos. In Palestine as well as in Egypt, the people who brought those features were foreign. They, and perhaps others, made their contribution to the culture of the country, but the basic way of life, for which the architecture, the pottery, and other material equipment is the best evidence, remained the same, and this was Canaanite.

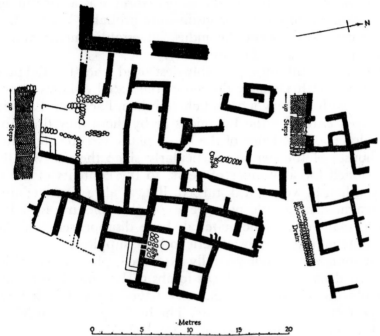

FIG. 39. Plan of Middle Bronze Age houses at Jericho.

Evidence for much of this comes from every site excavated in Palestine. But the most complete evidence comes from Jericho. This is not by reason of the buildings of the period exposed, for, as has already been said, the area in which the houses of the Middle Bronze Age survive is restricted. It shows (Fig. 39) a closely built-up area of rather small buildings, with narrow streets ascending the slope of the mound in a series of shallow cobbled steps (Pl. XXVII), streets such as those that could be found in many old Palestinian towns today. The houses lining these streets often had single rooms unconnected with any other part of the buildings on the ground floor (Pl. XVIII. 1), closely resembling the single-roomed shops in the bazaars today. Other of the

is an unjustified localization of a type of pottery found widespread in Palestine, Syria, Cyprus, and Egypt.

ground-floor rooms were for storage, and in some of these were found jars full of calcined grain, burnt in the final destruction of Middle Bronze Age Jericho.[1] In the area excavated by the 1957–8 expedition, in which was one of these storerooms with jars full of grain, the debris from the upper floor that had collapsed with the destruction contained twenty-three grinding querns, a number that could not have been for domestic use, and must indicate that on this upper storey was a corn miller's establishment, to which the grain store probably belonged. On the upper stories were the industrial establishments and the living quarters, as is the case today.

The burnt buildings, probably destroyed when the Egyptians of the XVIIIth Dynasty drove out the hated Asiatics early in the sixteenth century B.C. and chased them back into Palestine, destroyed either by the Egyptians or by those they drove out, provided good evidence of the house plans and the contents of the houses of the period, particularly since the site was then abandoned for a number of years, so the contents of the destroyed houses were not disturbed. But, as always, the contents of excavated houses do not give a complete picture, for all the objects made of organic materials have disappeared. This lack the contemporary tombs of Jericho have supplied.

For some reason not yet fully explained, physical conditions arrested decay in the rock-cut tombs of Jericho. The result is that objects of wood and basketry have survived in a fragile but perfectly recognizable state. The burial practice in Middle Bronze Age Palestine was that of multiple successive burials in what were probably family vaults. In the ordinary way each burial was placed in the chamber with accompanying grave goods. When the next burial came to be made, the space at the front of the tomb was cleared, and the earlier burials pushed to the rear, so that in due course a mound of jumbled remains, human bones and offerings, surrounded the latest burial (Pl. XXVIII. 2). In this pushing-aside process, fragile objects were carelessly and ruthlessly broken, as were the bones. The partly decayed objects of organic materials suffered much in the process. But in a small number of tombs some groups of burials, with the accompanying equipment, were found intact as they had been deposited; in most cases they belong to the very end of the Middle Bronze Age, and the burials, of complete family groups

[1] The interpretation of these as 'Palace Storerooms' (*LAAA* xxi) is certainly wrong, amongst other reasons because the so-called Palace is of a different period.

(Pl. XXIX. 1) whose members probably died within a short time as a result of some catastrophe such as a plague, preceded by such a short time the final destruction of the Middle Bronze Age town that the tombs were never reused.

In these tombs, therefore, were found in recognizable form the complete equipment that was considered necessary for the dead in after-life. Food was present in the form of complete or jointed sheep (e.g. at rear of tomb in Pl. XXIX. 1), in pomegranates and

FIG. 40. Reconstructions of table and stools from Middle Bronze Age tombs at Jericho.

grapes, drink, shown by intact skins left by the evaporating liquid, in great jars with dipper flasks suspended in their mouths (Pl. XXIX. 2). The almost universal item of furniture was a long narrow table, with three legs designed to allow it to stand on an uneven floor (Pls. XXIX. 1, XXX. 1, Fig. 40). The richer members of the communities had beds with a wooden frame supporting a string network (Pl. XXX. 1), and some also had stools (Fig. 40). More usually, the whole family lay and sat on rush mats (Pl. XXIX. 1). Nearly always the dead person was provided with a basket containing toilet equipment (Pl. XXX. 1); flasks of oil or perfume, wooden combs, wooden boxes with bone inlay, wooden dishes, (Pl. XXX. 1), bowls, juglets, and small boxes were other objects which have nowhere else survived.

The objects found were purely domestic and utilitarian. It is very noticeable that not a single object found suggests a religious use. It must be presumed that the Middle Bronze inhabitants of Jericho had some recognition of the existence of an after-life in this provision of equipment for the dead, but they seem to have had no feeling for the needs of the soul in this state, which is a remarkable contrast to the contemporary practice in Egypt.

It can, however, be accepted that the provision made for the material needs of the dead was that of the objects they had required during life. The equipment of the dead man is that of his household furniture during life, and it is on this basis that the reconstruction of a room in Jericho of about 1600 B.C. has been made (Pl. XXX. 2).

The period to which this room belongs is probably approximately that of the Patriarchs. The land through which these earliest Hebrews moved with their flocks and herds contained towns with houses like this, seen by them though they lived in tents. But more closely relevant to the background of Biblical history is the fact that, though Jericho itself was destroyed early in the sixteenth century and abandoned for a time, there is no break in culture between the Middle and Late Bronze Ages; the break is a convenient political one, but no more. The form of the pottery vessels (for which alone there is certain evidence) is modified, towns perhaps became less wealthy and less well-built, but this was the way of life that the infiltrating Israelites found, and which they adopted.

Thus archaeology shows that the Amorites of the Bible arrived in Palestine c. 2300 B.C. as nomads and destroyers of a pre-existing urban civilization. For perhaps four centuries they lived there, leaving little behind them except their dead in the tombs upon which so much labour was expended. In Syria their brothers and cousins had a similar way of life. But somewhere in Syria, probably centred on Byblos, an amalgamation of these nomads and the pre-existing, more civilized population took place, and out of this the Canaanite culture emerged. From this centre it spread throughout coastal Syria and Palestine, to re-establish an urban way of life. This way of life had a strong power of survival. It absorbed many new influences, such as that of a superimposed warrior aristocracy who surrounded the towns which they controlled with defences on a new plan and expanded their area, but the underlying culture remained. This culture the infiltrating Israelites found, and archaeology is clear that they adopted it; it was the cohesive power of their religion that caused them eventually to emerge from it as an entity that has contributed so much to humanity.

# INDEX

# BIBLICAL REFERENCES

PLATE I

1. A house of the Intermediate Early Bronze–Middle Bronze period at Jericho, with typical flimsy walls and irregular plan.

2. Burial in E.B.–M.B. Dagger type tomb at Jericho.

PLATE II

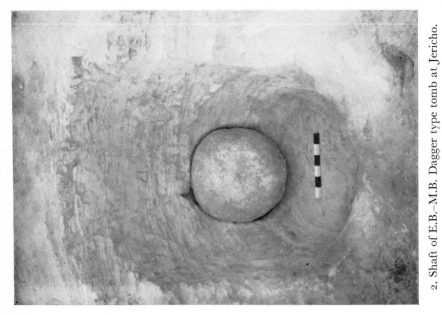

2. Shaft of E.B.–M.B. Dagger type tomb at Jericho.

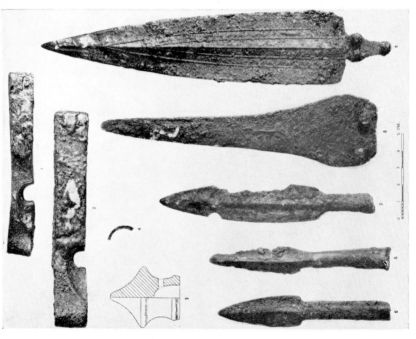

1. Weapons from the Middle Bronze I Tomb 911 D at Megiddo.

PLATE III

1. Shaft of E.B.–M.B. Pottery type tomb at Jericho.

2. Interior of E.B.–M.B. Pottery type tomb at Jericho.

PLATE IV

1. Pottery vessels placed with burial in E.B.–M.B. Pottery type tomb at Jericho.

2. Pottery vessels placed with burial in E.B.–M.B. Outsize type tomb at Jericho.

PLATE V

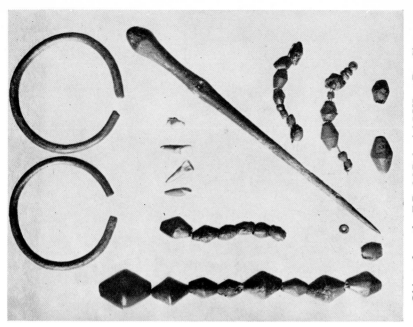

3. Objects from the E.B.–M.B. burial LXI at Ras Shamra.

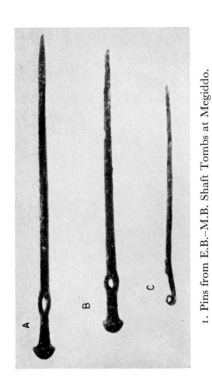

1. Pins from E.B.–M.B. Shaft Tombs at Megiddo.

2. Metal objects from Tomb 1101 B Lower at Megiddo.

PLATE VI

1. Air view of Ras Shamra

2. Air view of part of excavations at Ras Shamra

PLATE VII

1. Qatna, south rampart from S.

2. Qatna, south rampart, with modern village in SW corner.

PLATE VIII

1. Qatna, east rampart from E.

2. Interior of Qatna, with modern village on site of earlier tell.

PLATE IX

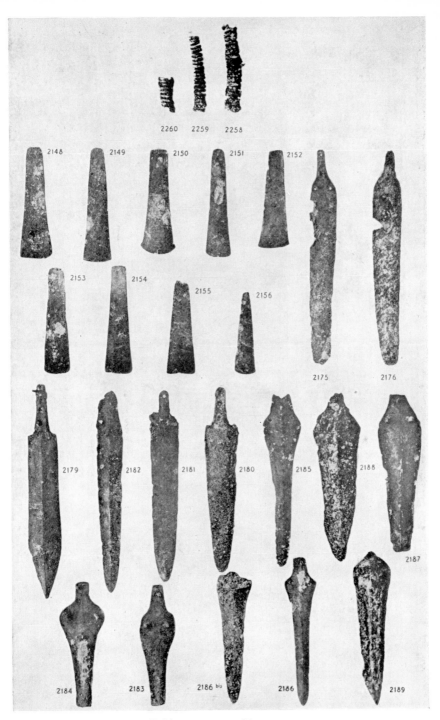

Byblos: contents of jar 2132.

PLATE X

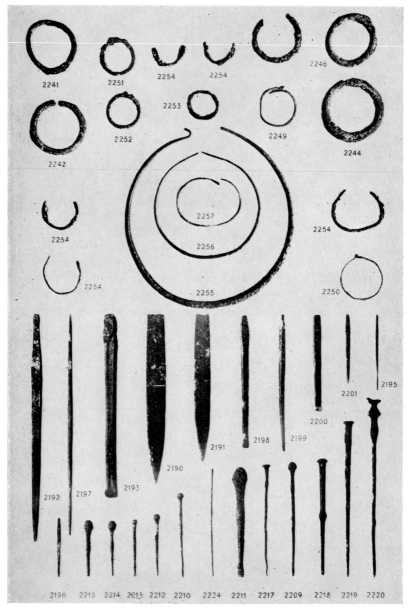

Byblos: contents of jar 2132.

PLATE XI

1. Byblos: vessels in bronze (1) and silver (2–3) from jar 2132.

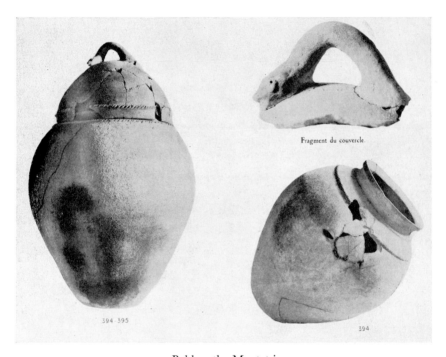

Fragment du couvercle.

394-395

394

2. Byblos: the Montet jar.

PLATE XII

Byblos: contents of the Montet jar.

PLATE XIII

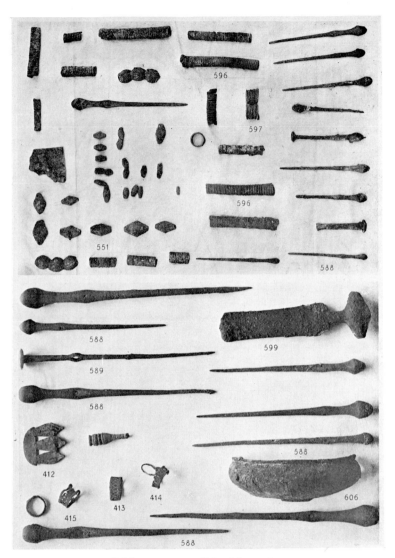

Byblos: contents of the Montet jar.

PLATE XIV

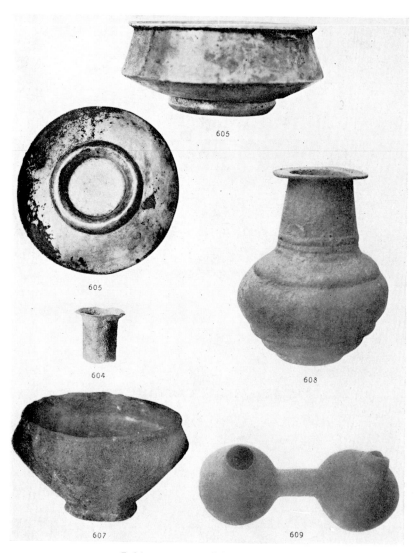

Byblos: contents of the Montet jar.

PLATE XV

2000

Couvercle de la poterie nᵒ 2000

2064

Byblos: foundation jars 2000 and 2064.

PLATE XVI

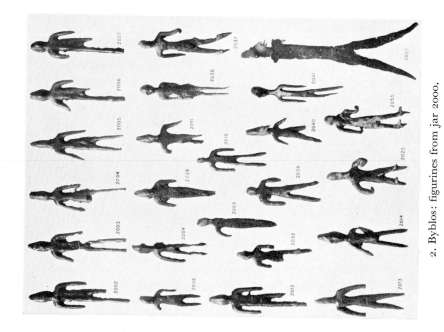

2. Byblos: figurines from jar 2000.

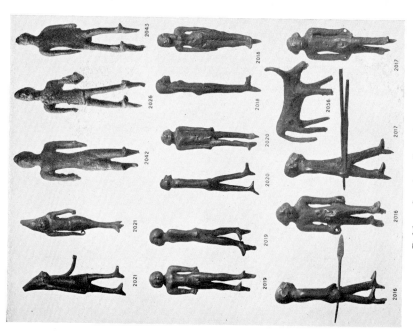

1. Byblos: figurines from jar 2000.

PLATE XVII

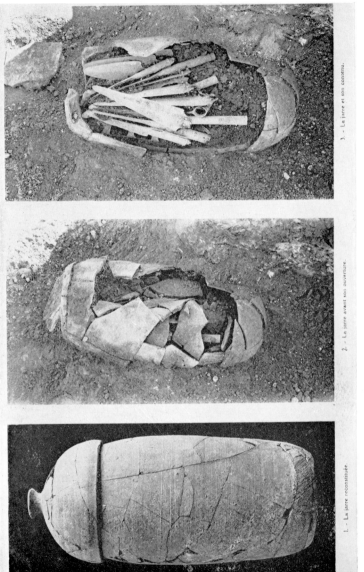

3. – La jarre et son contenu.

2. – La jarre avant son ouverture.

1. – La jarre reconstituée.

Byblos: deposit χ from the *Champs des Offrandes.*

PLATE XVIII

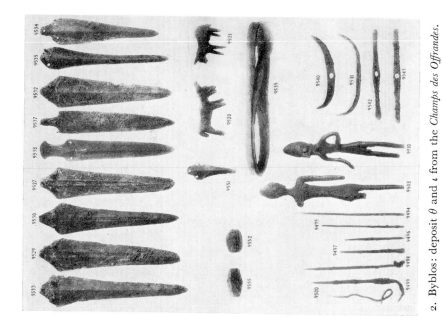

2. Byblos: deposit θ and ι from the *Champs des Offrandes.*

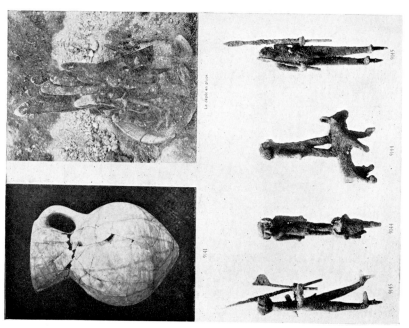

1. Byblos: deposit ζ from the *Champs des Offrandes.*

PLATE XIX

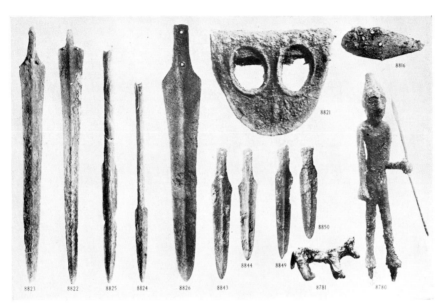

1. Byblos: deposit ε from the *Champs des Offrandes*.

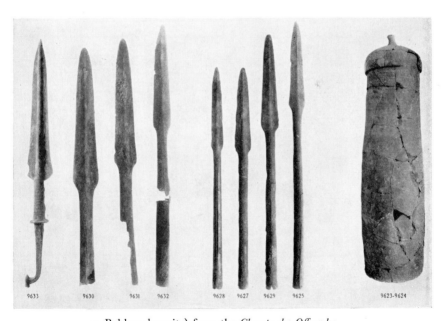

2. Byblos: deposit λ from the *Champs des Offrandes*.

PLATE XX

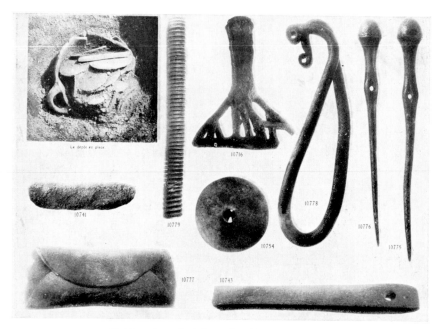

1. Byblos: deposit φ from the *Champs des Offrandes*.

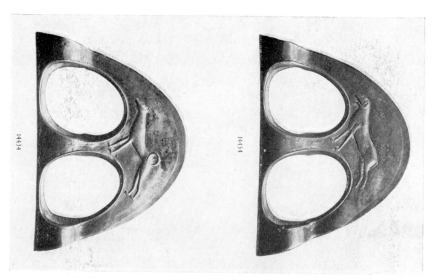

2. Byblos: fenestrated axe in gold from the Obelisk Temple.

PLATE XXI

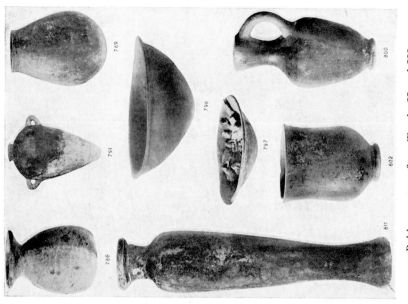

1. Byblos: pottery from Tombs II and III.

2. Byblos: pottery from Tombs II and III.

PLATE XXII

2. Plaster facing of M.B. rampart at Jericho.

1. Stone revetment at base of M.B. rampart at Jericho.

PLATE XXIII

1. Plaster facing of M.B. rampart at Jericho, showing keying into the bank behind.

2. Plaster facing of M.B. rampart at T. Duweir.

PLATE XXIV

1. Ditch and bank of M.B. defences at T. Ajjul.

2. Ditch and bank of M.B. defences at T. Fara.

PLATE XXV

Air view of Hazor.

PLATE XXVI

1. Air view of Khan Sheikhoun.

2. The ramparts of T. el Yahudiyeh.

3. The ramparts of Carchemish.

PLATE XXVII

Street in M.B. town at Jericho.

PLATE XXVIII

1. Street, with underlying drain, and houses in M.B. town at Jericho.

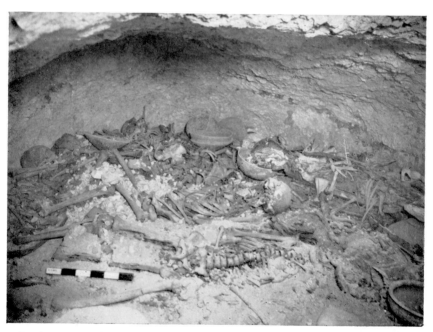

2. Typical M.B. tomb at Jericho, with final burial on floor in front, and skeletons and offerings of earlier burials piled round walls.

PLATE XXIX

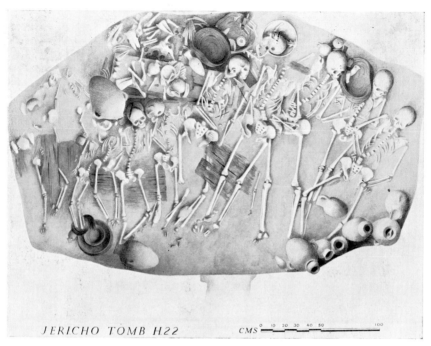

JERICHO TOMB H22          CMS

1. M.B. tomb at Jericho containing adults, adolescents and children, probably a family group buried simultaneously, with their funerary equipment.

2. Jar from Jericho M.B. tomb with dipper juglet suspended in mouth.

PLATE XXX

1. Skeleton in Jericho M.B. tomb lying on wooden-framed bed, with beside it a wooden table and on left basket with toilet equipment.

2. Reconstruction of a Middle Bronze Age room on the basis of evidence found in the Jericho tombs.

DATE DUE